THE TOTAL
CHRISTIAN
GUY

Phil Callaway

HARVEST HOUSE PUBLISHERS

Except where otherwise indicated, Scripture quotations in this book are taken from the Holy Bible, New International Version®. Copyright © 1973, 1978, 1984 by the International Bible Society. Used by permission of Zondervan Publishing House. The "NIV" and "New International Version" trademarks are registered in the United States Patent and Trademark Office by International Bible Society.

Verses marked KJV are taken from the King James Version of the Bible.

Verses marked NASB are taken from the New American Standard Bible, © 1960, 1962, 1963, 1968, 1971, 1972, 1973, 1975, 1977 by The Lockman Foundation. Used by permission.

Cover design by Left Coast Design, Portland, Oregon.
Cover photography by Ron Nickel Photography.

THE TOTAL CHRISTIAN GUY
Copyright © 1996 Phil Callaway
Published by Harvest House Publishers
Eugene, Oregon 97402

ISBN 1-56507-447-5

For my father, who told me stories.
And my brothers, who told me fibs.

Thanks

My wife, Ramona: For not taking certain parts of this book too seriously. You are the wings beneath my wind.

Stephen, Rachael, and Jeffrey: I wouldn't even trade you kids for a good night's sleep.

Mom: You are my number-one encourager. If every guy had a mother like you, the human race would be a little bit crazier and a lot better off.

My sister, Ruth: For only putting Vicks Vaporub on my eyelids once. For sensing early that I needed lots of prayer. And for doing something about it.

My personal psychiatrists: Vance, Ron, Chuck, James, and Monte: Let's hoist a ginger ale to "The Circle of Six" and long talks around the couch. I can't imagine spending Tuesday evenings with more intelligent, handsome guys. Oya. TGIT.

Bill Jensen and the staff at Harvest House: Bill, that was a cheap shot, and I think I owe it to you before I go any further to say that anyone who can ingest six hot dogs at a Colorado Rockies game and still make it to the parking lot should be able to handle cheap shots. Seriously, Bill provided much of the impetus for this book, his ideas were invaluable, his ingenuity an inspiration. He's my kind of guy. But that's no reason to dislike him.

Corporate sponsorship: Coca-Cola, for keeping me awake late enough to write. Tylenol, for keeping my children asleep. (Just kidding there. Please do not send me letters on this. I strongly recommend that you consume only recommended dosages.) Kirby Vacuums, for the complimentary shampoo of our sofa which lasted only seven hours (the shampoo, not the sofa). Without you this book would have been longer.

Frank King: For allowing me to tell our story. Keep seeking, not hiding.

Prairie Bible Institute: For throwing common sense to the wind and renewing my contract. Seriously, keep shaping lives—the world needs changing.

My Lord, Jesus Christ: The story of my life.

Contents

Contents

INTRODUCTION

Who, Me?

Writing books is easy work, let's face it. All you have to do is stare blankly at a computer screen until a great idea hits you. Or until drops of blood form on your forehead and you die of unknown causes. If you happen to be working on a book for Christian guys, the matter can be complicated even further.

For one thing, your wife wants to read each and every word because she highly suspects that the project may need minor revisions (such as the deletion of chapters 6 through 12—the ones which involve her).

"If you don't zap them," she tells you, holding a pair of sharp scissors in the vicinity of your computer cord, "I'll do it myself. Then you can spend the winter in the shed. I'm sure the kids will bring you scraps."

Of course, you think she is overreacting, perhaps from the stress of living with a writer, someone who:

a. Is periodically cranky.
b. Makes messes.
c. Experiences mood swings.
d. Eats at strange times of the day.

Come to think of it, that sort of reminds me of someone who was hanging around our house just before the kids were born.

I made the mistake of mentioning this to Ramona and adding: "Writing a book is the closest a guy will ever come to giving birth, you know."

Of course, I was right, but she didn't take it all that well, judging from how quickly the scissors moved.

Separating the Men from the Guys

Another problem with writing a book for guys is that people misunderstand you. They think you're writing a book for *men*. This is simply not the case. There are already an awful lot of men's books out there, and most of them are awfully serious. You see, thousands of men have spent the last ten years banging drums, plumbing the depths of their innermost feelings, and struggling to define terms like "patriarchal socialization" and "internalized domination." Whereas us guys have spent the last decade plumbing the depths of the grace of God, and struggling to define terms like "balanced schedule," "job security," and "spousal communication." Okay, we have also been fiddling with the remote control.

Recently I was researching this project by lying on the couch trying to forge my way through a book entitled *A New Christian Understanding of Manhood* (subtitle: "Shattering Patriarchal Paradigms and Rediscovering the Woman in You").

The book came with a complimentary bumper sticker: "SAVE THE MALES," and on page 16 when the author suggested that we return to a "deliteralized, deapocalypticized eschatology that harkens back to a tradition of individualized [yawn] feminine [yawn] masculinity [yawn]," I closed the book and stared at the ceiling as I wondered why we take ourselves so seriously.

I'm sure I could have come up with three or four good reasons had I stared at the ceiling long enough, and I suppose it didn't help that I was attacked by my two sons who wanted to play sock-hockey on the living-room floor. That's one of the problems with us guys. We're too busy living life to spend a whole lot of time analyzing it.

I'm not saying introspection and solemnity aren't necessary components of a balanced life, for we live in serious times. But one of the things I've learned during my short sojourn on this planet is that I am underqualified to stay serious very long.

I'm sure I could write a serious book about the problem, with a title like *Archetypes of the Capricious Soul: A Self-Analysis*, but I would probably start inserting subtle messages [Hey, guys!] along about chapter 2 [Lighten up!], and this would make sober readers extremely ticked off.

A sense of humor has a way of landing one in a fair amount of hot guava juice over the years, and I can't wait to tell you about it. But before we get to the stories, please allow me to get semi-serious.

One of my concerns in writing this book is that the cover contains a picture of my actual body placed near the word *total*. This was not my decision. We are still looking for the person who made this decision. Personally speaking, the only times I can remember my body and the word *total* being linked so closely are:

1. The time Mom made me tell Dad what I did to the car.

2. The day my third-grade teacher interrupted class to write my name on the blackboard, proclaiming in capital letters: "PHILIP RONALD CALLAWAY, SOMETIMES YOU ARE A TOTAL PAIN."

In third grade my vocabulary was not that wide, so I took it as a compliment. But as my years increased, as maturity threatened to set in, I discovered that *pain* was rarely a nice word, and that *total* meant "complete," "entire," and "absolute." I also realized that the fondness I once held for my third-grade teacher was beginning to wane.

Upon entering adulthood, I began to earn a living sweating at computer screens, and people liked what I'd written. So I decided to write a book for Christian guys. The title would be *The Total Christian Guy.*

After much thought and some insights from my pastor, my friends, and my wife, however, I decided there was a slight problem.

Here it is:

I am not the Total Christian Guy.

I am not even close.

If there's anything I've learned for sure since third grade, it is this: I am the biggest sinner of them all. Not a day goes by when I am not reminded of the fact. Not a day goes by when I don't fall short. If you bought this book hoping to read the advice of a guy who has it all together and remembers where he filed it, you'll be disappointed. If you were hoping for a 12-step recovery plan or a surefire guarantee, I apologize.

So, who then is this Total Christian Guy?

Simply this: He is one who takes Jesus Christ into every situation, every decision, every relationship. And when he falls short, he invites Him back the next time.

That's a lifelong process, isn't it? One that begins again every time you check into a hotel, speak to a neighbor, walk by a newsstand, or fiddle with a remote control. Each one of us is in process. That's what this book is all about.

If you could use a few laughs, if you would like to be reminded of the things that matter most, or if you want to hear again about a God whose grace is the wildest story of them all, I think we'll enjoy each other's company. You see, there is only one Total Christian Guy. And He's the story of my life.

Oh yes, one more thing: I sincerely hope you'll think of me with fondness while you're reading. Most of this book was written in our shed.

Phil Callaway
Three Hills, Alberta, Canada

CHAPTER ONE

The Total Christian Guy Quiz

The following quiz is designed to assist you in determining whether or not you qualify as a Total Christian Guy. It is not to be confused with other tests, such as the Taylor-Johnson Temperament Analysis which was used on the author in its developmental stages (the test's). Please answer the following questions honestly, bearing in mind that while you may not necessarily be graded on your answers, it would be a nice gesture if you phoned Mrs. Bittleston, your fourth-grade Sunday school teacher, and informed her of the results.

Important: This quiz should not be used for friendly wagering nor as ammunition during petty disagreements.

1. It's Saturday morning. Your wife asked you to move some furniture. Your best friend just called with free passes to the golf course. You will:
   a. Move furniture.
   b. Say, "Honey, I helped you move the checkered sofa in the middle of the night last Thursday, my back has not been the same since, and I will be glad to help you just as soon as wolverines become popular house pets."

c. Tell your wife you've just received an urgent call from your pastor, who is stranded in his '68 Oldsmobile on the interstate.

d. Negotiate.

2. You are attending your son's Little League championship. The score is 4-3 for the opposition. It's the bottom of the ninth, there are two outs, runners on the corners, and your son Billy is up to bat. You:

a. Wish you were at home whipping up a soufflé.

b. Shout words of encouragement. Words like "Duck, Billy, duck!"

c. Hurl peanuts at the pitcher, then blame small children around you.

d. Pray.

3. Your 14-year-old daughter asks if she can go on a date. You:

a. Explain to her that open communication, trust, dependability, and good character are the determining factors in such a decision; that when she shows all of these characteristics simultaneously and is mature enough to set an example for her little sister Helga, she will be permitted to take part in group dating, followed by double dating, both of which will prepare her for the responsibility of single-couple dating at a later time—when she is approximately 30.

b. Laugh uncontrollably.

c. Say, "Ask your mother."

d. Install land mines in the front yard.

4. Departure time for Sunday morning church has arrived, but your wife has not. She is still moving about the house and checking appliances—in spite of the fact that you are

once again late for church. While you wait in the car with the children, you decide to:

a. Return to the house and ask with sincerity, "Is there anything I can do to help you, Dear? I know I traumatized you this morning by bringing breakfast in bed a little late. I certainly do apologize."

b. Leave without her.

c. Return to the house and start World War III.

d. Go over the kids' memory verses with them and somehow resist the urge to honk.

5. Your wife finally makes it to the car, your faith in the miraculous is restored, and you are on your way to Grace Community Church. Suddenly, while you are making a crucial left turn, a Presbyterian brother noses in front of you with his '78 green Camaro and *cuts you off*. It's time to:

a. Recognize this as one of those rare opportunities life's classroom affords you to calmly demonstrate to the next generation that decency, brotherhood, and self control are not only admirable, but attainable virtues.

b. Follow him to the First Presbyterian Church parking lot and stuff a potato in his exhaust pipe.

c. Somehow find a way to blame your wife.

d. Go ahead and honk.

6. You are on your way home from the service, and your eight-year-old asks you, "Why, if Solomon was so wise, did he have so many wives?" You:

a. Go into a lengthy explanation of the cultural differences between ancient Israel and modern America, pointing out that many of the wives were merely tokens of the official policy of friendship and subservience between kingdoms, and that they may have been married without ever seeing each other.

b. Look for a green Camaro.

c. Say, "Ask your mother."

d. Admit that you don't have all the answers. But when you get home you're going to look into this one. Together.

7. After 13 agonizing years, you have finally reached the Annual Mixed Slow Pitch Church Softball Final. The rules require a minimum of two women to be on the field at all times. Five have shown up. You, the captain, decide to:

a. Sit on the bench, realizing that there are far more important things than baseball, that this could be a character-building event for all, and that each person should be treated as an equal, regardless of petty things like gender.

b. Hide their gloves.

c. Put three women on the bench, the fourth at catcher, and the fifth at second base where three guys can rescue her should something awful occur (such as a ball being hit in her direction).

d. Volunteer to sit on the bench and hope like crazy that one of the women says something.

8. You are on your knees giving thanks for the new purchase: a late-model minivan, complete with compact disk player. The phone rings. It is your 18-year-old son calling from Biff's Auto Repair to tell you that he has totaled the van. It's time to:

a. Total the telephone.

b. Ask if the CD player still works.

c. Ask if the other vehicle was a green Camaro.

d. Ask your son if he's okay.

9. Your life verse is:

a. Psalm 119:99 (KJV)—"I have more understanding than all my teachers."

b. 1 Corinthians 9:27 (NASB)—"I buffet my body . . . ," something you have been doing for years now at fine restaurants everywhere.

c. 1 Timothy 2:11—"A woman should learn in quietness and full submission."

d. Matthew 22:37-39—"Love the Lord your God with all your heart and with all your soul and with all your mind . . . and . . . your neighbor as yourself."

10. If asked, you would describe yourself as:

a. Witty yet articulate, intelligent yet vulnerable, a good listener, a good shopper, able to follow recipes, comfortable tossing salads, comfortable in your numerous roles.

b. Able to bag a deer at 200 yards.

c. Able to bag a deer at 200 yards. Blindfolded. With a blowgun.

d. Tired.

11. Your son Billy just hit a three-run homer to win the Little League championship. This is remarkable considering that you don't even have a son named Billy. But if you did, and he hit the game-winner, you would:

a. Faint.

b. Console opposing team parents by patting their backs and saying, "Hey, second place isn't all that bad."

c. Congratulate the umpire on *finally* calling a good game.

d. Run onto the field screaming, "That's my kid! That's my kid!"

How to Score: First of all, you have to be willing to give 110 percent. Then you take a pass at the 30-yard line, hurdle the linebacker, run like crazy, lunge over the goal line, then go completely nuts. Whoops! Wait a minute! That's the wrong kind of scoring. To see how you rate on "Total Christian Guy Quiz," give yourself one point for each time you picked "d," deduct one point for each time you answered "c," add one-quarter of a point for each "b" answer, and claim one-third of a point for each time you selected "a." If you are left with anything at all, this is usually a good sign. If you have taken the trouble to do this, you are an amazing guy. Most guys are already reading chapter two.

CHAPTER TWO

The Perfect Match

Whoever considers his own defects fully and honestly will find no reason to judge others harshly.

—Thomas à Kempis

It was one of those glorious and promising springtimes, when the Canadian winter finally hauls out a white flag and surrenders to the surging carpet of green (usually about mid-July). Barren trees regain their rightful colors. Furry woodland creatures wriggle out of hiding to stand blinking in the bright sunshine. Mr. and Mrs. Sparrow watch proudly as their offspring stand on tiny legs and jump from the edge of the nest, only to be eaten by Mr. Weasel, who has anticipated this moment all winter.

For most of us, however, it is a splendid time of year. And this particular spring, excitement was at a fever pitch. Revival, you see, had come to town.

It came unexpectedly while Mr. Janz[1] was trying to teach us fractions, and, appropriately, it came out of the east from a

---

[1] The best sixth-grade teacher I ever had.

place called Saskatchewan, which I had heard of but never seen. "Can anything good come from Saskatchewan?" someone asked. "I mean, don't they close the place on weekends?" The question, of course, was rhetorical. Something good *had* come from Saskatchewan. So good that it interrupted fractions for a full three days.

During most of that time, I sat on the back pew of our spacious chapel with fellow skeptic Steve Porr. He too had spent his first 11 years in religious situations. Weekends we faithfully attended Sunday school together. Weekdays we toiled tirelessly in a Christian school. We had been through some high times, the two of us, what with putting pennies on train tracks, cats in rain barrels, and pins in Loretta Hickok. But, as yet, the things of God had not held us quite so spellbound.

The previous day we had weathered the first wave of the revival—a day when "all heaven broke loose," to quote one impassioned teacher. The turning point had come when Miss Hale, the school secretary, went forward to give a short but memorable testimony, during which she invoked the memory of her tiny baby brother who had died when he was just about our age.[2]

"He was a lot like some of you," she said, her eyes roving over the rear pews. "Energetic. Vibrant. Full of life. A delicate

---

[2] Miss Hale, interim director of the Women's Christian Temperance Union and occasional substitute teacher, rarely spoke of the past without a great deal of emotion. If you were in her class and hadn't studied for an exam, it was possible to delay it indefinitely with questions such as, "Tell us about the time your grandmother was carried off by bandits during the Great Train Robbery," or, "What were you doing on December 7, 1941? I don't think it is a day which shall live in infamy. Do you?" Or, if you didn't know your history all that well and still longed to delay things, you could tell her that you had been reading your Bible and had come across the verse: "Drink no longer water, but use a little wine for thy stomach's sake," and you were just wondering what she thought.

flower in the springtime of life. A bud just longing to be a leaf. But one day he fell from a poplar tree, and the next thing I knew, he was looking up at me from a little white casket." Though she tried, Miss Hale could not finish, so the principal, Mr. Pike, gave the invitation for her, playing heavily on the imagery surrounding the poplar-tree incident. Most of the students went forward, but the two of us waited it out, our arms folded resolutely through all 11 verses of "Just As I Am."

I had come to regard Mr. Pike with a great deal of respect in recent days, and it had much to do with the fact that he had a daughter named Ruthie.

She was one year older than I and sat nearer the front of the chapel and off to one side. If I leaned hard to the right, I could see her cute blond curls just past the silver post which held up her side of the room. If I was real lucky, she would flick the curls and turn her head. I had been secretly in love with Ruthie Pike since she began wearing the new wire-rimmed glasses. Following a fourth-grade mixed ice skating party, during which I "reluctantly" held her hand, I sat down and penned a poem, spelling out my deep devotion to her. It was entitled "Ode to a Knife," and, if I recall correctly, it went something like this:

> Without your love, my life will be shorter,
>   Surely I think by at least one quarter.
> Unless you love me, I know I shall die,
>   This is the truth, Ruth, I tell you no lie.
>
> I'll slit my throat with a Swiss army knife,
>   And leave you there crying the rest of your life.
> For, after all, what's a guy without you?
> Just a big ugly sky without any blue.

I thought of putting a tune to it, but nothing seemed good enough for a piece of literary work which blended just the right amount of Shakespearean tragedy with my own heartfelt hope-lessness. I imagined myself bending on one knee as Ruthie read it. She would most likely pull out a hankie, wipe the tears be-hind those wire-rims, and faint into my waiting arms.

For some reason, though, I decided to show the poem to no one, relegating it to my school desk instead. That's where Raydean Keller happened to come across it one afternoon while I was up front sharpening a pencil. The poem became public domain after that, and for the next few days I enjoyed near-celebrity status. Fellow classmates turned to me during math class with their fingers down their throats, and when I walked down the hall, older boys stopped talking and made kissing sounds with the backs of their hands.

The intensity of my devotion remained undiminished, however, and I was keenly aware of the fact as I sat in chapel leaning hard to the right, my skinny arms folded.

A Reverend Albert L. Swanson was bringing the word that day. He kept one hand rooted firmly in the Old Testament, and the other he used for balance as he moved precariously about the edge of the platform.

"I know what you're thinking," he said, abandoning his notes for the conclusion. "Some of you are thinking, 'I'm a good kid. I don't make a lot of trouble. I go to church. I go to a Christian school. I memorize Scripture. I don't steal much. I don't smoke. I don't chew tobacco. I eat my vegetables.' But let me tell you something, pal. Goodness never got anyone into heaven. No sir. Goodness never impressed anyone up yonder. And goodness won't amount to a hill of beans if your life is snuffed out in an untimely accident and you go straight to hell." Some of the smaller children squirmed at his lan-guage, but Reverend Swanson wasn't through.

"I'm asking you to get out of that pew and come to the front. I'm asking you to turn your back on yesterday and open the door to forever. I'm asking you to bring your sin to the altar and lay it down. Come. Come now as we sing."

You didn't dare whisper between the verses. Tension hung in the room like the calm before a downpour. I sat quietly, listening for the pitter-patter. Wondering who would be the first drop. Yesterday Beth Freeman had started it, a mere trickle at first then a raging deluge, but today it could be anybody. Anybody, that was, except me.

I wouldn't be going forward.

Not after what happened a month ago.

It was a Sunday evening after church. March was almost over, but winter had yet to raise the white flag, so Steve Porr and I walked home backward into a nippy east wind. From the parking lot, exhaust fumes rose heavenward like Old Testament sacrifices. "Take a last look before the Tabernacle burns down," said Steve. We laughed, and I started thinking about how much fun it would be to light the match, to wield such power, and I wondered what I would do on Sundays afterward, with all that free time.[3]

The next morning, while Mr. Janz was pointing out that verbs and nouns were not synonyms, there came a timid tapping sound at the classroom door. A college-aged gentleman

[3] Steve and I liked matches a lot. We liked the smell of them in the box, the feel of them in the hand, and the miraculous *swish* they made when friction caused a combustible mixture to burst forth miraculously into flame and we were left holding a tiny torch and endless possibilities. Once, after reading a child-rearing book, my mother made me spend a whole Saturday afternoon in the backyard lighting a box of 500 matches, one at a time. "Let each one burn down slowly, then blow it out," she instructed, reading aloud from the book, knowing I would be cured once and for all and would never touch another one. But I loved every minute of it and was disappointed when the box ran dry. Matches were the only thing that ever made me want to major in chemistry.

with frightened eyes was ushered into the room and stood off to one side, surveying the class. We surveyed him back. Finally his eyes landed on me and Steve. "That's them," he said, raising his eyebrows. "That's them," he said, retreating from the room. Mr. Janz eased his top teeth over his bottom lip and slowly shook his head. "Come with me, fellas," he said.

I had been to The Office on previous field trips, so I knew the place well. A large Travel France poster with the *Arc de Triomphe* had always clung to the north wall. I noticed with disappointment that it had been replaced by a delicate watercolor, probably etched by someone's relative. One year ago, when I was asked to bend over, hang onto my shoes, and take it like a man, I had gazed back between my pant legs, found that Arc, and although it was upside down and a little faded, I had taken refuge there. Today there was only a small painting of a cold winter landscape. Today there was no place to hide.

"Ah, fellas, fellas," Mr. Janz began soberly, still shaking his head. "This is a sad, sad day for me."

"Um . . . I'm sorry," I said, quite sincerely.

"It's not that you've been such outstanding students or anything," he continued, scanning us for the first sign of a crack, "but I know your parents. They're such fine people. I . . . I just can't believe it was you."

"*What* was us?"

"That did it."

"That did what?"

"That did *what?* Oh, fellas—"

"But . . . we don't know what you're talking about."

"Do you have any matches in your pockets?"

"Um . . . no."

There was a pause as he looked us over carefully, tapping his knuckles gently with a #2 pencil.

"Last night two boys forced their way into the Tabernacle. They went into the men's restroom and lit it on fire."

"Lit it on fire?" We stood in unison, hoping we didn't look more surprised than we ought to have been. "Lit it on FIRE? You're kidding."

"No, fellas. I am not. Please be seated."

"Well . . . did it . . . you know, burn down or what?"

"No, fellas. A security guard arrived just in time and hosed down the blaze before it could threaten other parts of the building."

"Whoa. That's a relief, eh?" said Steve. "Well, I guess we should be getting back to class now."

"Fellas, I've been informed by a young man in the Bible college that he overheard one of you saying, 'Take a last look before the church burns down.' Is this indeed true?"

I looked at Steve, wondering if he really had the nerve to do something I could only dream about. Oh, I knew he didn't like Sunday school much either, but I never thought he would be able to muster this much courage.

Steve was looking at the icy window—an arsonist studying frost formations. At last he broke the silence: "Yes, that was me."

I exhaled slowly.

"But I didn't light fire to nothin'," he continued. "Honest, we were just watching the smoke come up from the cars—that's all. It looked kind of cool, like the church was on fire or something. But I didn't do nothing wrong, honest. You've gotta believe me, I cross my heart and hope to die, I—"

"Steve—" Mr. Janz rarely interrupted, but this was one of those times. "Where were you last night about ten o'clock?"

"Um . . . in bed sleepin'."

"Could anyone substantiate that?"

"I can," I said with sincerity, but with limited knowledge of my verbs. "I was sleeping too."

Sitting in the chapel listening to the singing, I knew that no one would ever believe us. Mr. Janz hadn't said much since our morning conversation, and I noticed that he had taken home some of his favorite houseplants, perhaps rescuing them from a possible inferno. Occasionally I sensed his suspicious gaze when I was looking down at my books. Even classmates seemed to view Steve and me with suspicion. After all, the criminals had not been apprehended, and no one could remember anyone being called to The Office under stranger conditions.

"We hear you like fire a lot," said Valerie Carlson, a mean-faced, freckled girl who sat behind me and liked to speak in a singsongy voice. "Everyone knows you did it." For someone so young, Valerie had extremely bad breath, like she'd been rooting around all weekend in compost. But what really burned my toast was the fact that I was feeling guilty—something Valerie would have liked very much.

Oh, it wasn't that I had started the fire. It was that I had wished it so, and I got to wondering if in the end there was really any difference.

The rains had begun, and I felt like I was drowning. One of the Honecker boys had been the first to fall, and from there the rest went down like dominoes. I was leaning hard to starboard during the final verse, searching for an anchor in those blond curls, when suddenly I noticed that they were not there, that Ruthie had carried them to the front and placed them on the altar. It was then that the tears started, and I couldn't get them to stop. Unfolding my skinny arms, I stepped overboard and waded to the front.

Fittingly, Mr. Janz was my counselor. We sat in the grade eight classroom together. I liked the feel of the desks. They were large, spacious, easy to slump in.

"Philip, do you have anything to tell me?"

"No. I mean . . . yes." I sat up straight.

"Well . . . ?"

"A lot of the time I have bad thoughts."

"Aha. And do you do anything about these bad thoughts?"

"Sometimes. But mostly I just have them."

"Do you think about *burning things?*"

"Ya. Sometimes."

He sat still for a moment, studying my face. Then he opened a well-marked King James Bible to Romans 12:1,2 and read to me:

I beseech you therefore, brethren, by the mercies of God, that ye present your bodies a living sacrifice, holy, acceptable unto God, which is your reasonable service. And be not conformed to this world: but be ye transformed by the renewing of your mind, that ye may prove what is that good, and acceptable, and perfect, will of God.

"Have you done that, Philip?"

"Pardon me?"

"Have you given Jesus your thoughts, your mind?"

"I think so. I've memorized those verses."

"But you must do them," he said. "It won't get easier as you get bigger, but you can start controlling what goes into your mind today. It will make tomorrow much brighter indeed."

When we finished praying together, he looked at me and said, "Are you *sure* you don't have anything else to tell me?"

"I'm sure."

"Is everything okay?"

"Yes," I smiled. "I'm fine." And for the first time in three days, I meant it.

Epilogue: Steve Porr also received counseling that day. He, too, was found guilty of lesser crimes. To this day the other criminals have gone undetected. Ruthie Pike moved to the state of Washington, where the winters were not so harsh. I believe she married a poet.

Study Guide Questions

Be Honest

1. When you were in sixth grade did you ever beat up a kid who wrote poetry? Okay, seriously, were you ever accused of something you didn't do? How did you feel?

2. What is one thing you'd love to do if you knew you wouldn't get caught?

3. Did you ever envy the testimony of one who had committed worse crimes than you? What separates you from them?

4. Do you find yourself talking about the sins of others? Why?

5. Charles Swindoll said, "Oh, how horrible our sins look when they are committed by someone else." What do you think of his statement?

Go Deep

1. Can you identify with the words, "A lot of the time I have bad thoughts"? What do you do with your bad thoughts? Read Romans 12:1,2 again. Now, read it again, but this time turn it into a prayer.

2. Spend time thanking God for His mercy.

3. Find a favorite CD or cassette with a song about God's grace and mercy. Listen to it alone. If you feel really inspired, write a poem. Be careful who you give it to.

This righteousness from God comes through faith in Jesus Christ to all who believe. There is no difference, for all have sinned and fall short of the glory of God, and are justified freely by his grace through the redemption that came by Christ Jesus.

—Romans 3:22,23

CHAPTER THREE

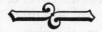

The Battle of the Bald

*Contentment is a pearl of great price, and whoever procures
it at the expense of ten thousand desires makes a wise and a
happy purchase.*

—John Balguy

In case you haven't heard, there are now eight wonders of the
world:

1. The Hanging Gardens of Babylon.

2. How many people buy lottery tickets.

3. The Mausoleum of Halicarnassus.

4. That I can find anything in my shed.

5. The Statue of Zeus at Olympus.

6. That my wife can find anything in her purse.

7. The Great Pyramid of Giza.

8. The rate at which I am losing hair.

Oh sure, if you look at the cover of this book number eight appears to be under control. But that's because they glued ferret fur to my head before the photo shoot. Just kidding, but the truth is I'm 34-years-old and already my hair is going underground and coming out my nose.

If you're one of those guys who still has his original hair, go ahead and laugh. A few decades of psychological help and I'll get over it. But if you're experiencing a recession yourself, if you've been shedding on pillows and clogging drains, if you've stopped combing and started rearranging, you'll be happy to know that there is hope. Unfortunately, I can't think of anything remotely hopeful right now, but I'll try to think of something. While I do, let's look at some ways in which the scientific community, working hand–in–hand with laboratory rats and medical researchers, has shown us just how bleak the picture really is.

1. **Genes.** Scientists recently announced that they have discovered the gene that causes baldness. As you might expect, this caused a flurry of excitement within the genetic community, until one of the researchers—a completely bald guy who had vengeance on his mind since earning the nickname Ultra Ban way back in his twenties—sneaked into the laboratory under cover of darkness and smashed the gene. Do not give up hope, though. They have begun searching for another one.

2. **Mice.** An Associated Press report claims that scientists have taken a first step toward treating baldness and gray hair by implanting genes in mice. How did they do this? Well, it's really very simple. They enclosed the genes in tiny bubbles of fat and spread them on shaved mouse skin. As fat is able to penetrate almost anything, the tiny bubbles worked their way into the skin's microscopic hair factories and the genes began to activate and good things began to happen. Unfortunately,

guys, I still don't take much comfort from this. Sure, it worked on mice, but when was the last time you saw a bald mouse?

3. *Drugs.* If you were alive during the '60s, you know that drugs taken in large quantities helped men forget many things, including their baldness. But this was momentary and, let's face it, the side-effects were monstrous.

Researchers now claim, however, that they have found a proven hair-growing drug. It's called Minoxidol and it has been known to work on various objects: Fruit, ivory, snooker balls. What these same researchers won't tell us, however, is that Minoxidol will probably not work on *you*. That's right. It has been largely ineffective in men. And what they will *definitely* not tell us is that it works for women—whom other researchers have conclusively proven do *not need it*.

4. *Music.* After years of research and very little success, the Daiichi Pharmaceutical Company, a leading Japanese drug maker, decided to make wads and wads of money by releasing a compact disc of Mozart music. Yes, believe it or not, the CDs are now marketed exclusively through pharmacies. Daiichi Pharmaceutical claims that the music will soothe the listener, relieve stress, and even reverse the balding process. I'm not sure about this, but they may be on to something here. You see, during high school I conducted similar experiments on my father in which I played loud music for him. This caused his head to *appear* hairier.

Practical Tips to Try at Home

Relocate. Yes, you may want to move to another state where no one will recognize you—where no one will know that you once had hair. Wait a minute, that's not what I mean! What I mean is relocate your hair. Move it from an area where it thrives to The Dead Zone. If you have small children, they will be happy to do this for you some Saturday morning while you are resting.

Surgery. If you would like to take part in a less painful procedure, you can make an appointment with a skilled surgeon who will be glad to put you to sleep, insert individual hairs into pinholes made with hypodermic needles, and charge you approximately $10,000,000 while the anesthetic is wearing off. Unfortunately, you may have to part with even more cash once the hair surrounding the transplants begins to fall out.

Innovate. The most popular technique that I personally know of is to grow your hair very long on one side and comb it carefully over the deceased area. My father does this as well as anyone. The beauty of it is that if you have false teeth to go along with it, you can scare the living daylights out of your grandchildren during a windstorm.

If none of this works for you, wear a hat everywhere. Glue it on, if necessary. Or grow your eyebrows to their full length and comb them back. This method is still in the research stage, so let me know how it goes.

Coming Out on Top

I was standing out at shortstop the other day, watching ground balls zing past. My hair was blowing away in the breeze, and I didn't have the energy to chase after it. Suddenly, a comforting thought hit me: *Our heads were made for something else. They were made for more than growing hair.*

When it comes right down to it, we determine very little of what goes on above the hairline. But we can do something about what goes on *inside* our heads. Second Corinthians 4:16

says it best: "Though outwardly we are wasting away, yet inwardly we are being renewed day by day."

Wasting away, all right. My calculator informs me that if all goes well, I have another 40 years to live.[1] That's 14,600 days. Or 350,000 hours. Or 21,024,000 minutes. Since the average human breathes 14 times a minute, I have roughly 294,336,000 breaths left. Less if I forget my wife's birthday.

Without being morbid, allow me to say that it's a good idea to number our days. To realize that unless Christ returns first each one of us will be history one day. More than ever, it is my desire to live every day, every minute, every breath, for the glory of God.

How about you? Will you spend your life concerned with the right things? Are you being renewed day by day? Are you content with who God made you? With what He's given you? With what He's doing *inside* your head?

Two hundred years ago, when my own father had all his hair, Johann Wolfgang von Goethe wrote out nine prerequisites for contented living. Whether you're the eighth wonder of the world or not, these are the things that really matter.

1. Health enough to make work a pleasure;

2. Wealth enough to support your needs;

3. Strength to battle with difficulties and overcome them;

4. Grace enough to confess your sins and forsake them;

5. Patience enough to toil until some good is accomplished;

6. Charity enough to see some good in your neighbor;

7. Love enough to move you to be useful and helpful to others;

[1] Even less when you consider that I often fly on airplanes which were built by the lowest bidder.

8. Faith enough to make real the things of God;

9. Hope enough to remove all anxious fears concerning the future.

If you're still not convinced, you may want to try one more suggestion: Shave off all your hair, leaving yourself completely bald, and looking like you did it on purpose. This was done effectively by Kojak and Mr. Clean, so it may work for you.

Make sure you use a good sharp pair of scissors. If you can't find them, look in your shed. If you still have trouble, ask your wife. They're probably in her purse.

Study Guide Questions

Be Honest

1. Are you balding, wrinkling, sagging, or aging in any visible way? Was the best thing about reaching your current age the realization that you won't die young? Are you able to smile about your age? Why or why not?

2. The seven stages of a man's life are spills, drills, thrills, bills, ills, pills, and wills. At which stage are you?

3. If you could change one of your physical attributes, which would it be? Why?

4. What is your contentment level? Are you more concerned with what goes on inside your head or outside?

5. They say the average life expectancy for North American guys is 72 years. If you haven't surpassed that yet, how many more years do you have to go before you beat the average? (Feel free to use a calculator if you need to!) In

one sentence, what would you like to accomplish for God in the remaining years?

6. Winston Churchill once said, "I have only managed to live so long by carrying no hatreds." What kind of old man would you like to be? What will it take to achieve that goal?

Go Deep

1. Begin praying about your future. Ask God to renew your mind day by day.

2. Go over Johann Wolfgang von Goethe's list again. Pray through it, asking God to work in you in each of these nine areas.

3. Read Psalm 90:12; Isaiah 46:4; and Proverbs 16:31. When you have time read Gordon MacDonald's *The Life God Blesses* (Thomas Nelson Publishers).

So we fix our eyes not on what is seen, but on what is unseen. For what is seen is temporary, but what is unseen is eternal.

—2 Corinthians 4:18

CHAPTER FOUR

Opening Address to the Federation of Christian Guys

(January 24, 1996)

Mr. Chairman, distinguished guests, paying members of the federation, those who got in for free, guys of all ages:

During the last few years it has been my privilege to address numerous women's groups all over our fair country. I have always considered this a real honor (as would a sparrow were he asked to sing before the opening kickoff of the Annual Meadowlark Convention), but I must confess, I always consider it a bit ironic, too. You see, back in high school, back when I lay awake nights hoping girls would call and ask me to speak with them, they would not give me the time of day, nor would they return my calls. (*Laughter.*) But now that I am a happily married, middle-aged, balding sparrow, they phone all the time and ask me to sing for them. Now, don't get me wrong—as a gender we would be miserable and possibly even extinct without women, but this weekend I'm glad to be with a bunch of guys. (*Applause.*)

I don't know about you, but I feel like I've just come through a nine-day week. I have a book due at the publisher in two weeks. A magazine due in three. A wife due in four. I'm just kidding about the last item. My wife says I can go ahead and have more children, only I'll have to fill out the adoption papers. And look for someone to raise them.

I love kids. We had three of them in three years, and the whole experience was a lot of fun. For me, anyway. When someone asks my wife what it's like to have three kids in three years, she claims she is far more satisfied than the man who has three million dollars. How so? "Well, the guy with three million wants more." (*Laughter.*)

Years ago, before expectant fathers were allowed to faint in delivery rooms, three guys were waiting for the joyous news. Nervously, they sat in the waiting room, thumbing through magazines, chewing their nails, looking down the hall for the first sign of activity. Finally, a nurse arrived, informing the first man that his wife had just given birth to twins. Excitedly, he told the others, "Isn't that ironic? I pitch for the Minnesota Twins!"

A few minutes later the nurse returned and informed the second man that he was the proud father of triplets. "Wow!" he exclaimed. "What a coincidence! I work for the 3M Company!"

The third man slammed down his magazine, panicked and raced for the door.

"Hey, what's the matter?" called one of the others.

"I work for 7-Eleven!" he yelled. "I'm outta here!" (*Laughter.*)

Can you identify? Do you feel like heading for the hills? Psalm 46:10 says, "Be still, and know that I am God."

It's tougher than ever to obey.

A few nights ago I was ironing shirts when my father dropped by to remind me that times have changed.

"When I was your age," he said, peeling off his gray fedora and easing himself into a soft chair, "I enjoyed being a man. Oh sure, life wasn't beachfront property then, either. There were pyramids to build, dinosaurs to avoid, and fire to invent. But at least we had clearly defined roles. Not anymore. Not you guys. No sirree."

He sniffed the air. "Speaking of rolls, are those cherry tarts done yet?"

"Not quite," I said, holding a shirt up to the light with a critical gaze. "They need another ten minutes. I always put the cherry ones on 350°, you know. The crust is flakier that way." (*Laughter.*)

"Flakier, alright," he said softly, hauling both feet onto a stool. "You know, I wouldn't trade places with today's guy for a doctorate in Home Economics. No way. I get tired just watching you."

I creased another collar, listened to his laugh, and wondered if he had a point.

It was the first thinking I'd done in a while, what with attending church planning sessions, babysitting during Ladies' Night Out, driving kids to sporting events, hollering at insurance salesmen, and . . . oh yes, holding down a full-time job.

You know the feeling: You make breakfast for some hungry children, kiss your wife good-bye, remind her to come home after work, clip coupons, leaf through recipe books, consider calling in sick, and it isn't even Tuesday.

Maybe Dad was right. After all, most guys I know are so tired they can't even work up a good yawn. Oya? (*Cries of "Oya!"*)

Back in fourth grade, being a guy seemed like a fine option. This was the year Mr. Kowalski handed out those little forms asking us to check the appropriate boxes so we could be registered with the government. For the first time in my life, I faced some tough decisions, as you can see from this overhead:

Who Are You? A Simple Test.

(Please print. Last time you didn't do this, and we still
don't know who you are.)

1. What is your full name? _____
   (Hint: Your mother calls you this when she is really
   mad.)

2. Where do you live? _____
   (Please do not describe the house or the people who live
   near you. Just give us your address. Please spell it right
   this time.)

3. Are you: ☐ M or ☐ F?

The first two I had no trouble with. The first two I
breezed through. But when my pencil arrived at question
three, it hovered there with uncertainty. Was I M or F? It
was up to me.

Those who ticked F were destined to spend gym class
prancing around trying to look interested in basketball. Those
who selected M could ram Wally Akers into the end wall
while he attempted a lay-up.

The decision wasn't even close.

But on the other hand, I knew that girls had always had
it easier. Girls got to stay home where there was food,
warmth, and meaningful conversation. Boys were herded
outside to shoot each other in imaginary wars and to spend
hours arguing over who died first. Girls received more
Christmas presents, more understanding, more innate social
skills. Boys received more chores, more spankings, more gas.
(*Audience reaction.*) Girls are smarter than boys. They know
everything about boys. All boys know about girls is that they

desperately want one. This is not rocket science. A fourth grader can tell you this.[1]

Still, in the face of such knowledge, I lowered the pencil and drew a bold X beside the M.

A few nights ago, I was holding an iron and wondering about my decision.

"Did you hear about the Egyptian guy who asked Pharaoh for time off to attend childbirth classes?" Dad was interrupting my thoughts.

"No," I said, "Was he flogged?"

"Close. He became ancient history."

I managed a polite smile, donned my oven mittens, and withdrew the tarts. "Let me tell you something, Dad. We guys today have biblical reasons for the way we are."

"You do?"

"Sure," I mused. "Uh . . . let me see. . . . You remember Moses, right?"

"Sure do. He led the Israelites in their exodus from Egyptian slavery and oppression."

"That's right. But did you ever wonder why he wandered in the wilderness for 40 years?"

---

[1] Guys have no problem understanding this. When I share this at men's retreats, they salute during this paragraph. They use one simple word: "Oya." Women don't do this. They use words like "Yaright," and they capitalize each of its letters for emphasis. After this story appeared in the newspaper, I received mail from females. They wanted my street address so they could come torment my dog, dent my hubcaps, and pelt me with petrified tarts. Tarts baked at 450°. I told them we reside at 911 Tulsa Avenue, Boston. (If this is a real place and you live there, I apologize. I was too tired to think up a more generic address.) Ironically, I've spent years writing sensitive articles for women. Still, one lady wrote: "I have always viewed you with suspicion, knowing that if you were pushed to the limit, if you were forced to make a decision, you weren't really one of us after all. Deep down inside, you are a guy."

"That's easy. It was because of his unbelief."

"No. Try again."

"Because he wanted the Children of Israel to really appreciate the Promised Land once they got there?"

"No. The truth is, it took them so long because Moses refused to ask his wife for directions." (*Laughter.*)

"Okay," Dad said, hauling his feet onto the chair again, "you got me there. But are there any other examples?"

"Sure, there's . . . um . . . there's Noah. Most of us remember him as a good and righteous man, the father of Shem, Ham, and Japheth, but how many of us know that he was also the founder of the Christian Guy Movement? Aha. You had no idea, did you? But it's true. One morning Noah woke up, fixed himself some breakfast, and said, 'Honey, I'm outta here. I've gotta work on that big boat.'

"Mrs. Noah whirled around, a screaming child in one hand, a sharp wooden fork in the other. 'What about the kids?' she growled.

"'The kids? They can ride in it once I'm done,' replied Noah, gathering his robe and assorted primitive tools.[2] But Mrs. Noah wasn't through. 'Do you think I'm gonna be stuck in this hut all day with *all this screaming?*' she screamed, moving slowly towards him.

"'But dear,' replied Noah, 'Sweetheart. Lamb Chops. Certainly you don't expect me to . . . to help out with the children. I'm 500 years old.' Mrs. Noah was inching closer. '*I think I'll go nuts,*' she said, with a crazed expression.

"So it was that Noah agreed to let the kids come along. For the next few hundred years they helped him at the office, and Noah became someone every Christian guy could look up to. A sensitive listener. A peacemaker. A guy who could tell you a thing or two about quantity time."

---

[2] Including the stone power drill.

"I always wondered why the ark took so long to build," said Dad. "You've sure cleared things up."

We laughed a bit, then sat in silence, munching cherry tarts.

"They sure are flaky," said Dad.[3]

Then he handed me some free advice: "There are a thousand voices shouting for your attention, son. Don't miss the most important One. God asks that you act justly, that you love mercy, and that you walk humbly with Him. You do that, and everything else will fall into place."

Then he pulled on the gray fedora and headed for the door.

I glanced at my watch. It was nine o'clock already. I hadn't even started the laundry. (*Audience reaction.*)

Study Guide Questions

Be Honest

1. Patrick Morley, an international speaker, says, "If I were limited to making only one observation about men today, it would be that everywhere I go I find that men are tired." Do Morley's words describe you? Or are you too worn out to understand the question?

2. What do you like about being a guy these days? What don't you like? Are you tired of being all things to all men? To all women?

3. In 1894, Agnes Repplier wrote, "It is the steady and merciless increase of occupations, the augmented speed at which we are always trying to live, the crowding of each day with more work than it can profitably hold, which has cost us, among other things, the undisturbed enjoyment of friends. Friendship takes time, and we have no time to give it." What has your pace of life cost you? Is it worth it? If not, what can you change?

[3] I've received numerous requests for my cherry tart recipe. I've included it at the end of this chapter!

4. Do you find that projects and prestige are sometimes more important than people? If so, should you be making some changes in this area?

5. What should you be saying no to?

Go Deep

1. Ask your wife, your child, or a friend if they think you're too busy. Talk with him or her about what you could eliminate from your life.

2. Sit down and take inventory. Ask yourself about each major activity: Why am I doing this? Will this matter one year from now? Five years from now?

3. Read Psalm 127; Ecclesiastes 2:22-26; and Matthew 6:25-34.

4. Memorize the following verse:

He has showed you, O man, what is good. And what does the LORD require of you? To act justly and to love mercy and to walk humbly with your God.

—Micah 6:8

Real Flaky Cherry Tarts

Bottle of Coke	A teaspoon
Bag of chips	A cup
Ice	An oven
Water	A bowl
Flour	

1. Preset oven to 350°.

2. Pour a tall glass of Coke over ice.

3. Sample it.

4. Stick some flour in a bowl.

5. Pour water over it.

6. Mix till real sticky.

7. Put more Coke in your mouth. Add chips.

8. Get some small boxes or cans from the cupboard where your wife gets stuff when she bakes.

9. Take heaping teaspoons from three or four of these containers and dump them on the sticky stuff.

10. Stir till it's not quite so sticky.

11. More Coke, chips.

12. Find some cherries (you might have to ask your wife where these are).

13. Eat some. Paste the rest to the stuff that used to be sticky.

14. Bake until flaky.

15. More Coke. More chips.

Feeds 2–12, depending on how fussy they are.

CHAPTER FIVE

Confessions of an Overpaid Referee

Decisions of the judges will be final unless shouted down by
a really overwhelming majority of the crowd present.

—Rules of the first open boomerang
tournament at Washington, D.C., in 1974

Many years ago, when the polar ice caps were receding and professional athletes played for love of the game, I became an ice hockey referee. To this day I'm not entirely sure why. Perhaps I entertained some admirable urge to facilitate hours of enjoyment for youngsters needful of positive male role models who would instill within them Strong Character, Camaraderie, and a Sense of Fair Play. Or maybe I just wanted to hear their parents scream, *"Kill the ref! He has no friends."*

Nevertheless, I was sworn in on a snowy day in late October, unaware that the following irreversible laws of the universe were already in motion:

Rules for Referees

a. Yes, you were sworn in on opening day, but this will not be the last swearing you hear.

b. Your eyesight, good looks, and family history will often be called into question.

c. When you are right, no one will remember.

d. When you are wrong, no one will forget.

e. You will find officiating much like standing between two famished five-year-olds with a solitary ice-cream cone.

f. Thousands of people still appreciate the following poem penned 100 years ago by an anonymous irate fan:

> Mother, may I slug the umpire?
> May I slug him right away?
> So he cannot be here, mother,
> When the clubs begin to play?
>
> Let me grasp his throat, dear mother,
> In a dear, delightful grip,
> With one hand and with the other
> Bat him several on the lip.
>
> Let me climb his frame, dear mother,
> While the happy people shout,
> I'll not kill him, dearest mother,
> I will only knock him out.
>
> Let me mop the ground up, mother,
> With his person, dearest do,
> If the ground can stand it, mother,
> I don't see why you can't, too.

On Friday evenings, certain church teams would offer me 10 dollars to sneak out of youth group and referee their games. Over the years I earned 1,640 dollars, minus expenses, which I kept careful track of, for income-tax purposes. I'm not sure what it is about church games which brings out the worst in a man, but one night, while trying to separate two ministers who were exchanging verbs which had little to do with the Five Points of Calvinism,[1] it occurred to me that I should have been paying them. After all, while my friends were singing "Kum Ba Ya," I was learning the following principles which would shape my life and the balance of this chapter.

1. *Mankind is basically evil. Womankind, too.*

The doctrine of original sin was much easier to grasp after the normally placid Mrs. Thomas—who as far as I could recall had never said an unkind word while teaching our Sunday school class—booed, hollered, and pelted me with snowballs.

I have also watched grown men spit on one another, bite each other, break each other's bones, and engage in activities which are illegal as well.[2]

---

[1] One pastor informed me (I kid you not!) that when he stepped on the ice, he left Jesus behind. I'm not sure if he felt Jesus couldn't handle a contact sport, but you could definitely tell the guy was playing without divine guidance. Unfortunately, I didn't have the wisdom to ask him if, when he went on business trips, he forgot he had a wife.

[2] For those of you who are unfamiliar with the sport of hockey, I defined the game this way in *Daddy, I Blew Up the Shed*:

> The word *hockey* finds its origins in a combination of the North American Indian word *tamahakee*, or "to chase with great speed," and *splochet*, French for "to bludgeon." It is a team sport played on a slippery surface with sharp blades, sharp sticks, a dangerous projectile called a puck, and not nearly enough padding. It is also the only legitimate sport since Roman rule which permits its participants to shish kebab opponents and, if caught, be made to spend two short minutes in a penalty box thinking about doing it again.

2. *Life is not fair.*

Please see previous point.

3. *Tough times have their advantages.*

During my high-school years, refereeing was the only way I could get girls to chase me. They chased me down darkened corridors, out into parking lots, and sometimes out of town.

4. *Men and women are different.*

I believe it was the great American philosopher Yogi Berra who, just before being impaled on the tongs of a fork, quipped, "Women tend to be dispassionate when it comes to sports." Psychologist Dave Barry seems to agree. "Women as a group," he wrote, "have a long way to go before they reach the level of intensity and dedication to sports that enables men to be such incredible jerks about it."

At the risk of being impaled myself, allow me to say that I think Yogi and Dave were on to something here. I mean, let's be honest. The average woman probably couldn't tell you that Lou Gehrig hit 23 grand slams during his 16 seasons with the New York Yankees. Or that the shortest major league player was Eddie Gaedel, a 3-foot 7-inch, 65-pound midget who pinch hit for the St. Louis Browns on August 19, 1951, wearing number ⅛.[3]

My own wife, for example, was not even watching the World Series this past fall—if you can believe that—choosing instead to do things like communicate with our children. One survey indicates that the only women paying any attention at all were the players' mothers, and even they were talking on the phone at the time, saying things like, "Sports is a foul ball in the line drive of life."

[3] When asked about it, Bill Veeck, Baseball Hall of Famer, said, "My epitaph is inescapable. It will read, 'He sent a midget up to bat.'"

Of course, some mothers break this rule. My wife's interest in sports actually increased when my son began playing soccer this year. But her knowledge of vital aspects of this complex game is limited, judging from her cheers: *"Kick it! Kick it!"* and, *"I said kick it, for Pete's sake!"*

I sincerely hope she stays away from snowballs.

5. *Nobody likes to lose.*

During my short career as a referee, I discovered that most dads want their kids to win far worse than the kids do. In fact—and this is a personal observation, so please do not hurl things at me—if given the opportunity to choose between World Peace and cheering their son to victory, most dads would want to know whether it was a preseason or a postseason game. (Alright, I'm exaggerating here. Not all dads are like this. Some just sit there, glaring from the bleachers, and thinking: *The ref's a necessary evil. Like the fumes that follow a jet.*)

6. *Occasionally there are exceptions to the rules.*

My friend Cory (who agreed to let me tell you this providing I didn't mention that his last name is Edwards), after seeing several good psychiatrists, was finally able to recall the opportunity he had to win the big high-school basketball game.

With no time remaining on the clock, and his team trailing by one point, Cory was handed the ball and a chance to send the game into overtime.

Mothers held their breath.

Fathers prayed, some for the first time since Easter.

Cory remained calm, however. A study in concentration. A picture of confidence.

Then he launched a shot which is still discussed at parties in his hometown. A shot which missed the net. A shot which missed the backboard. Yes, Cory hit nothing but wall.

He could have been lynched that night, had he not fled the building immediately. He could have given in to despondency, had his father not found him and done the best thing possible: He put his arm around his son—and started to laugh.

Thankfully, Cory joined him.

I'm wondering what it would be like if our arenas were packed with more guys like Cory's dad.

Guys who realize that life's biggest victories are seldom posted on scoreboards. Guys who come to encourage, not to live their dreams secondhand.

I, for one, might take up officiating again. Of course, I wouldn't skip out on youth group. I'm way too old for that.

Study Guide Questions

Be Honest

1. When you attend a spectator sport are you more exciting to watch than the game? Why?

2. Are your kids involved in sports? If so, are they glad when you come to watch?

3. What have you learned about yourself while playing or watching sports?

4. Major league batting champion George Brett once said, "If a tie is like kissing your sister, losing is like kissing your grandmother with her teeth out." Do you share George's sentiments? In the heat of the moment, what will you give up to win?

5. Do you find yourself debating the refereeing after a game? Why?

6. Duane Thomas, Dallas Cowboy running-back sensation, said during the 1970 Super Bowl week, "If this was the

ultimate game, they wouldn't be playing it again next year." Do you have his perspective?

Go Deep

1. First Thessalonians 5:11 says, "Therefore encourage one another and build each other up." What are some ways you could do this as a father? As a fan? As a husband?

2. Actress Celeste Holm once said, "We live by encouragement and die without it—slowly, sadly, and angrily." Ask yourself: Is anyone walking lighter because of what I said to them today?

3. Do you think we could use a few more guys like Cory's dad? Ask yourself: How could I be more like him?

4. Pray for your kids' coaches. After your child loses, sit down and tell him or her about the time you lost a big game.

5. Sometime, if you get the chance, officiate a game. Forego the pay—believe me, you'll learn enough to make it worthwhile.

Whatever you do, do it all for the glory of God.

—1 Corinthians 10:31

CHAPTER SIX

Till Rust Do Us Part

*Drive-in banks were established so most of the cars today
could see their real owners.*

—E. Joseph Cossman

It is a frightening thing to awaken one Sunday to find that
toddlers have discovered your car. The red one. The one that
never had a scratch. Until today.

"An elderly lady owned her," Honest Ed had informed me
on a cloudless day the previous summer, while gently caress-
ing her contoured roof and adjusting his purple suspenders.
"She only drove it Sundays, you know. Between the church,
her heated garage, and the car wash. Changed the oil after
each drive. Triple-undercoated the body. Kept plastic on the
seats. Heh, heh, this baby purrs like a Swiss watch. Ticks like
a pacemaker. And it's all ready to go. Of course, I'll top up the
tank before you take it."

Ed looked like he'd just stepped off a bad television ad;
nonetheless, I squinted at the paint job and thumbed the

corners of my Visa card. I hadn't taken her for a spin yet, but already the wheels were turning.

This was the kind of machine that fate has you meet once in a lifetime, and you fall in love immediately, vowing to be true the rest of your days, or until rust separates you. And if for some reason you are an idiot and don't buy it right now, you wake up in the middle of the night, cold and sweating, kicking yourself in the wallet, hoping fate hasn't picked someone else, and wondering if you should just hobble on down there right now in your Galaxy 500 and sit on the dream until Honest Ed arrives and ties the knot.

"As it is, I'll only be makin' 25 bucks on the deal," said Ed. "It'll go toward crutches for the twins, should they survive the surgery. We've gotta get 'em separated, you know. They're Siamese." A tear wound its way down Ed's pudgy cheek and splashed lightly on his tangerine tie.

There are times when life hands you an easy choice on a silver platter. This was one of those times.

After a short test drive and a long chat with my wife, I bought the car—hook, line, and cruise control. As I eased her out of the lot, Ed gently patted the hood and said good-bye, much like you would if your best friend had just climbed aboard a rowboat and was pointing it toward Italy. "I sure will miss her," I heard him say.

Each Saturday I polished that red Ford.

The chrome rivaled sunshine in those days. We planted tomatoes near it, and they grew fat from the rays. On Saturdays my neighbor Vance would come by to sample the tomatoes and annoy me. "Polishing the tin god, eh?"

I chuckled above my irritation. "Just being a good steward, that's all," I would say. *He's jealous,* I would think. *I don't blame him. How can you blame a guy who's still making payments on a rust-colored '66 Chevy Impala?*

About this time my wife began having children. They came one at a time, unlike Honest Ed's, but as they started to toddle, they would occasionally get together in bunches and hang out near my bright-red Ford. This was rarely good news for anyone, least of all the Ford. Sometimes Siamese children aren't the only ones who need separating, you know.

On that fateful Sunday just before the morning worship service, I opened the front door to find Rachael and Jeffrey standing upon the hood, smiling at me. They were two and one, respectively, and both were proud owners of sizable rock collections. Apparently they planned on bringing the collections to church, perhaps to put them in the offering, until they were sidetracked by a better idea: *What about we place these atop the shiny red thing and dance on 'em? Maybe we could change it into a two-tone. Maybe we could change Dad into a towering inferno.*

"It's just a car," said my wife as we drove to church, the smell of smoke lingering in the air. The blaze had been extinguished, but a little breeze could stir up the embers. After all, my investment had been devalued, my equity diminished.

"How can you say that? *Just a car*. It's not *just a car*. It's . . . it's—"

"Just a car," she interrupted. "Hey, be glad the car didn't decide to trample on the kids."

I wasn't so sure.

Upon reaching the parking lot, I was smiling at other parishioners, but my words were stumbling through clenched teeth. "Look at it this way," I said. "What if the kids scratched your . . . your . . . vacuum cleaner or something? Or . . . damaged one of your plants? Or ripped one of your new dresses?"

"They have, Phil," she said, waving kindly to someone. "By the way, what did you do with the kids?"

I don't know if your pastor reads your mail. Mine does. Of course, I don't have tangible proof of this, but even if he doesn't, I highly suspect that our cordless phones are on the same frequency, or that Pastor John is spending a significant percentage of his minister's salary on high-tech surveillance equipment which he zooms in on my car, because almost every Sunday he seems to delight in nailing me to the wall.[1]

On the morning in question, I sensed he was up to his usual tricks when he had us stand during the offering, then reach forward to the person standing in front of us and pull out a wallet. "Now," said Pastor John, "open it and give as you've always longed to give, but felt you couldn't afford."

Okay, I'm making this part up. But, I kid you not, his topic that Sunday was materialism, and he opened with an amusing anecdote to get the attention of those who were reading the church bulletin.

"Once upon a time a young man proposed to his girlfriend as they sat looking out over a glassy lake. 'Darling,' he said, 'I love you more than anything else in the world. Oh, I know I'm not wealthy. I don't have a yacht or a Rolls-Royce like Zippy Robinson, but I do love you with all my heart. Will you marry me?' She thought for a minute and then replied, 'Oh, Bobby, I love you with all my heart, too. But please, tell me more about Zippy.'"

I can't remember how he tied this in to the rest of his sermon, but before long he was reading from 1 Timothy 6, and I knew I was in trouble.

> But godliness with contentment is great gain. For we
> brought nothing into the world, and we can take

---

[1] I find this to be a very sad commentary on contemporary sermon preparation, and I plan to speak with him about it some day.

nothing out of it. But if we have food and clothing, we will be content with that. People who want to get rich fall into temptation and a trap and into many foolish and harmful desires that plunge men into ruin and destruction. For the love of money is a root of all kinds of evil. Some people, eager for money, have wandered from the faith and pierced themselves with many griefs. But you, man of God, flee from all this, and pursue righteousness, godliness, faith, love, endurance and gentleness.[2]

Pastor John didn't end there, so I picked up the bulletin again and tried to drown out the remaining verses by thinking about auto repair shops and doing mental calculation exercises. The problem was, I couldn't concentrate on anything but the last few verses.

Tell those rich in this world's wealth to quit being so full of themselves and so obsessed with money, which is here today and gone tomorrow. Tell them to go after God, who piles on all the riches we could ever manage—to do good, to be rich in helping others, to be extravagantly generous. If they do that, they'll build a treasury that will last, gaining life that is truly life.[3]

The next thing I knew, the pastor was quoting Martin Luther, "'I have held many things in my hands, and I have lost them all; but whatever I have placed in God's hands, that I still possess.' It's funny, isn't it," asked Pastor John, "North Americans possess more things than any other people in the world. We also have more books on how to find happiness."

[2] 1 Timothy 6:6-11.
[3] 1 Timothy 6:17-19 (The Message).

I was listening now.

"If you hold the things of this world too tightly, you will spend your whole life making only a snail's progress toward the Creator," he said. "Things must never fill the place God was meant to be."

I folded the church bulletin and looked up. I think Pastor John was looking right at me.

When we reached the car, I wasn't smiling.

"I guess I have some things to learn," I told my wife. "I guess anything we don't give to God has a way of possessing us."

She smiled in agreement. And watched me reach for the car keys.

It was time to let the kids out of the trunk.

Study Guide Questions

Be Honest

1. Humorist Billy Boswell said, "Nothing gives a used car more miles per gallon than the salesman." Have you ever been taken for a ride?

2. What was one model of car you loved in high school? Have you seen one lately?

3. Would you say money has been your servant or your master?

Go Deep

1. The experts tell us that the average American is exposed to 1500 commercial messages every day. I have no idea how they arrived at this, but the point is that we are inundated with materialistic messages. Are you doing anything about it? With your kids: try poking fun at TV ads sometime; come up with a few of your own; and discuss the impact ads have on all of us.

2. Ask yourself: Who or what would be hardest for me to give up? Sincerely offer that person or thing to God.

3. Go through the story of Abraham and Isaac in Genesis 22. Ask yourself: "What did God really require of Abraham?" Does this apply to you, too?

4. Fred Allen said, "I don't want to own anything that won't fit into my coffin." Reflect on his words.

My most cherished possession . . . is my faith in Jesus Christ, for with Him and nothing else you can be happy, but without Him and with all else you'll never be happy.

—Patrick Henry (1736–1799)

CHAPTER SEVEN

The Age of Enlightenment

*Part of the problem in trying to control population in the
Third World is that it is against the people's religion to use
preservatives.*

—College student in an essay

I was in fourth grade when I first heard about sex. For all I
know, it may not have existed before that point in history
(October 16, 1969—a Wednesday, I believe). In a rather memorable moment, a neighbor boy whom we shall call Bobby[1]
told me all about it. As I recall, Bobby had the whole thing
embarrassingly backward, and I trust that he has been informed of this, particularly now that he has his own counseling ministry.

Thinking back, I suppose I should have known that this
other dimension existed, for there were clues all along the way.
Earlier that same year, for instance, Jennifer Lynn Watkins
stood before our class, her long black hair nervously twirling.

---

[1] Because that is his name.

"My aunt won't be having any more kids," she informed us. "Her tubes are tired."

Mr. Kowalski almost injured himself, he was laughing so hard. But the rest of us didn't get the joke. Except for Priscilla Grundy. She pretended to know everything.

When I was 12, my mother attempted to broaden my horizons by interrupting a perfectly good baseball game for a straightforward discussion of the birds, the bees, and other assorted insects.

Although some of the details are a little sketchy now, I do remember sitting upon our plaid couch, baseball mitt in hand, thoroughly amazed at Mom's frankness.[2] In less than 20 minutes, my normally reserved mother told me:

a. Where I came from.
b. How I got there.
c. That it was all a part of God's marvelous plan, carrying with it rules that, when followed, would lead to a lifetime of freedom and fulfilment.
d. To, for goodness' sake, stop picking my nose.

Let me assure you: Coming from a Presbyterian, the first three points were well worth listening to.[3]

"Philip," she said in conclusion, "sex is a beautiful gift that God has set aside for husbands and wives. Don't you ever forget that."

I sat, wide-eyed, staring at the baseball glove. I was sure I wouldn't forget it.

---

[2] You must bear in mind that in those days the only ones speaking openly on this topic were also inhaling large quantities of banned substances.

[3] In subsequent years, I asked my father why he wasn't the one to inform me about this delicate topic. He said he thought Mom would do a much better job due to the fact that the only sex education he received came from an aunt who told him, "Sex is a filthy, rotten, and disgusting thing. Save it for the one you marry."

"Do you have any questions?"

I did have a question. In fact, for about 20 minutes I had been overcome with a desire to ask something of great importance. Finally I voiced it: "Um . . . may I go play baseball now?"

Moments later I was heading back to the diamond, smacking my glove and thinking: *There must be a better way to reproduce. If ever I have children, I'm sure I shall have found it.*

I called Mom today to remind her of The Talk. She's 72, and, like Mr. Kowalski, she laughed until it wasn't so funny anymore. Then she reminded me that they didn't have 100 zillion child-rearing books available to tell them how to pass on all the delicate details. And she added, "You live in a very different world, son. We pray for your children every day."

It's a different world alright. And sometimes it's a scary one. Wherever our kids turn—school, television, the video or convenience store—they are inundated with flashy signs pointing them in the wrong direction. Christian parents can no longer afford to remain silent. Nor can we limit sex education to The Talk.

At our house, opportunities to discuss the topic arrive unexpectedly. Just yesterday, Jeffrey and I were out in the yard when two flies came by, cruising at rather low altitude and in startlingly close formation. "Daddy," said Jeff, "they're getting married." We laughed together and had a brief chat. It was nothing new. From the time he was four or five, we've had many such impromptu conversations.

Of course, this whole thing can be carried too far:

Son: Dad, would you pass the sunflower seeds, please?

Dad: You know, Billy, you were once a seed.

Son: Well then, please pass the chips.

When I presented my son Stephen with his very own copy of an illustrated children's Bible, I had no idea just how illustrated it was. On one page there's a picture of Bathsheba bathing while David leers from a distance. Apparently, the artist ran out of the fig leaves which are usually strategically placed on such artwork.[4] Stephen came across the picture one evening, so he asked me, "What's going on here?" Fifteen minutes later, after I had given him The Talk, after I had informed him that the baby conceived that night died and that David lived in agony until he experienced God's forgiveness, Stephen turned the page, looked at another picture, and said, "What's going on here?"

I have tried to make it clear by my words and actions that in our house no question is taboo. But let me tell you, by the time he finished reading Song of Solomon, I was getting downright fatigued.

Seriously, it's important to remember that the dispersement of information is a small part of education. You see, you can have all the knowledge in the world, but without wisdom it can be dangerous.

When I think back to the night my mother interrupted the baseball game, it amazes me that this is the only time I can remember talking with my parents about sex. Yet somehow they managed to raise responsible, reasonably well-adjusted adults. How? I believe the reason is simple: Dad and Mom cared for each other. They provided us a lifelong demonstration of morality in action. By their tenderness and commitment, they showed us that the best sex education in the world is a mom and dad who love each other.

---

[4] If you are considering rushing out to find a copy, please carefully examine your motives.

Believe me, you don't take such things lightly. Especially when all you started out with was a fourth-grade education.

PS: By the way, I never did find a better way to reproduce. Not even close.

Study Guide Questions

Be Honest

1. Can you remember when you first heard about sex? (If you haven't heard about it yet, please write to me. I'll send you some pamphlets.)

2. Did Mom or Dad ever sit you down for The Talk? (If you can't remember, chances are they didn't.) Did you pass The Talk on to your kids?

3. *Men's Health* magazine predicts that "all the available information since the beginning of time will double over the next three years." Do you think, generally, that we are better off? Why?

Go Deep

1. Do you agree that we can no longer limit sex education to The Talk? Why or why not?

2. Do you agree that "the best sex education is a mom and dad who love each other?" Why or why not?

3. Gilbert West said, "Example is a lesson that all men can read." What are some ways you have failed in this area? Some ways you have succeeded? What are some practical things you could do to be a better example before your children? Before friends? Before your community?

4. What frightens you about raising children in these turbulent times?

5. Right now, take time to pray for your kids.

A teacher affects eternity; he can never tell where his influence stops.

—Henry Brooks Adams (1838–1918)

CHAPTER EIGHT

Aunt Gertrude

*To fall in love with God is the greatest of all romances! To
seek Him is the greatest of all adventures! To find Him is the
greatest human achievement!*

—Raphael Simon

When I was a child of seven or eight, life was an illustrated
adventure book just begging to be opened. I would wake
up each summer morning, eat a hearty breakfast of crackling
cereal and real cream, chase it down with burnt toast and real
margarine, rush out the door smacking my lips, then quickly
retrace my steps and pull on my jeans.

My older brothers liked me a lot in those days—so much
so that they even had a special nickname for me—a small
token of their deep admiration and respect. The name, to be
specific, was Aunt Gertrude, and they said it came from Latin,
although I didn't even know where that was. But who cared?
According to them, the name meant "Adventurous One," and
that was good enough for me.

Apparently, Tim and Dan spent a great deal of time searching for just the right name, but they finally discovered it while the Hardy Boys were chasing a runaway fugitive through a damp forest. In the encroaching darkness. Under a full moon. Surrounded by booby traps. Down to their last match.

Joe Hardy, blond and 17, turned to his handsome elder brother Frank, blinked his flashlight twice, and whispered wistfully, "What I wouldn't give for one of Aunt Gertrude's cherry pies." Those were very possibly the last words the tousle-haired youth ever uttered, because suddenly, before Frank could even remind Joe that Aunt Gertrude had been kidnapped in a previous adventure and had not been up to baking since, a gloved hand holding a shiny object shot through the dense underbrush and conked Joe over the head. He slunk to the forest floor, unconscious, his eyes fluttering helplessly in their sockets, like those bumper boats you find at water parks.

"Hokey Dinah!" exclaimed Dan, slamming the book shut. "That's it. We'll call him 'Aunt Gertrude.'" And they did, despite my parents' strong recommendations to the contrary.

Mom and Dad, you see, had higher hopes for me.

And although I'm sure they examined the Bible carefully, they were unable to find any biblical basis for calling me Gertrude.[1] "We named him Philip for a reason," they said, the reason being Acts 8:35, which read in those days, "Then Philip opened his mouth, and began at the same scripture, and preached unto him Jesus."

"That's all we want for our youngest," I heard them say. "May he preach Jesus."

---

[1] Dad even came up empty-handed after studying the original German.

But I had plans of my own. I much preferred Gertrude to Philip. Gertrude spoke of adventure, of dense forests and conquering heroes, of the sweet unknown. Philip spoke of . . . well, of things biblical, and just how exciting could that be?

As summer turned to fall, and my brothers' thoughts turned once again to goodwill, they determined not to let it end with name-calling. And so, during those times when they were feeling ill or had prior commitments, they graciously afforded me the opportunity to do their paper route. Once, when I had accumulated a full 30 days' worth of work, they handed me a shiny copper nickel, a soda-powered plastic submarine, a package of Black Cat firecrackers, and the glowing compliment, "Well done." But I would like to think my motive was not the money, the gifts, nor the accolades. No sir, I operated out of a sense of gratitude. After all, hadn't they given me the new name: Gertrude the Adventurous?

"Hey, Gertrude[2]," they said one day, while clutching their stomachs on the living room floor, "do you mind . . . just this once more . . . we're feeling really the pits . . . and, oh, yes, *watch out for Henderson's dog.*"

My parents must have been elsewhere at the time because the boys were listening to Elvis Presley sing "I Did It My Way" at 100 decibels. *Ha,* I thought, *he'll never make it anywhere with a voice like that. But I like the words. In fact, that can be my theme song.*

---

[2] Over the years the name changed from Aunt Gertrude to Gertrude to just plain Gerd. Former friends of mine still use it. Mr. Arthur Rashleigh, my grade eight teacher, even went so far as putting it on my report card. Mother was not amused.

Humming the tune, I went to the fridge and put something in my pocket, gathered a few things from a box beneath my bed, hopped aboard my purple two-wheeler, and took off, wondering at the strength of my brothers' laughter.

The Hendersons were largely responsible for the high rate of turnover in our town's newspaper and mail service departments, and their latest acquisition had done little to squelch the rumors. In fact, their new pet had sparked a rash of drive-by deliveries and some unpleasant exchanges on the bench in front of Red's Cafe.

"That there family is clearly breakin' the law," lamented Les Wiens, a short, stalky fixture who chain-smoked cigars fastest when he was talking. "They should be ashamed of theirselves."

But Jack Thiessen who hated cigars but loved good disagreements, felt otherwise. "They've had some bad experiences with Amway salesmen, that's all," he insisted. "They're merely taking the necessary precautions."

But the rumors didn't end at the coffee shop. Perhaps the most plausible was started by a Mrs. Flemmer, who insisted the Hendersons were within their legal rights, having been issued a special permit to conduct medical research on animals in the dead of night. Animals not normally seen outside the zoo. Animals best viewed from a car. Or with powerful binoculars.

Rancid, the family's current experiment, was nicknamed Houdini for it lacked the ability to stay in solitary confinement—something neighborhood cat owners were keenly aware of. The dog liked cats, it was said—really liked them in fact—preferring them to freshly ground beef.

"A bunch of little kids are missing too," said Jimmy Crites, a tall, narrow kid who seldom lied without good reason. "You couldn't get me to deliver a casserole there if the whole family was sick. Somebody's gotta do something."

I was that somebody. Tonight I would do something. As a result, I would be a local celebrity. Maybe national. I would go on all the talk shows—a remarkable feat when you consider that this was before talk shows.

Pedaling slowly toward the Henderson house (my last stop on the route), I tried not to miss any puddles, wondered all the while if Rancid was chained, and marveled at the growing sense of excitement which welled within my tiny body. I'd been writing a song recently, and I sang it loudly to give me courage:

> Hey ya hey hey,
> It's been quite a day,
> Oh ya hey hey,
> It sure has been.[3]

Taking a deep breath, I increased my speed. Until now, I had been guilty of drive-by deliveries. Of tossing newspapers from outside the Henderson's fence. But not tonight. Tonight I had a plan. Tonight I would hand deliver *The Herald*. After all, I was Gertrude the Adventurous. A 200-pound dog was just the challenge I needed.

Now you must understand that the idea of a morning paper had not yet reached our small town; therefore, delivery was carried out in the evenings, usually around dusk. And so, as darkness snuffed out the last rays of twilight, I quietly

---

[3] One of the better songs to emerge from the '60s.

leaned my bike against the peeling wood fence of Rancid's next-door neighbors, the Paynes,[4] pulled my coat about me, and removed the one remaining newspaper from the bag.

In the Paynes' front yard stood a weeping willow tree even older than their house, its long, sturdy branches out-stretched to the neighbors on either side. I had little trouble scaling the fence and even less climbing the tree. From there it was a short shimmy east on the largest branch of all: the one which snaked into the Henderson's yard and dangled a mere three feet above Rancid's doghouse.

The hound was over by the flower bed sniffing at something when I arrived, but when I whistled, it didn't take him long to find me. His huge body shimmered in the porch light as he gal-loped, drool cascading down his neck and across his shoulders. He was below me now, glaring upward. And growling.

I shuddered for a moment, then smiled.

"Here, boy," I called. "I've got something for you." Reach-ing inside my coat, I extracted a short stick of orange cheese, tied it to the ball of string, and lowered it to him. Growling, he inhaled the cheese, then shook his head hard. I yanked the re-maining string back up, and ducked to avoid the drool.

"Want another one?"

He did. So I lowered it to him. Then another. And another. Rancid appeared to be thoroughly enjoying himself, thinking that perhaps he had made himself a lifelong friend—one who would stick by him despite some of the nasty habits he had acquired. Like his penchant for cats, his trouble with drooling.

And then I produced the firecrackers.

The huge animal cocked his head to one side as I struck a match and lit the long fuse which held the firecrackers to-gether. Rancid licked his chops with anticipation as I lowered the flickering surprise.

---

[4] Who had no large pets, but could tell you a thing or two about nicknames.

Questions for Group Discussion

1. When you were a child, did you ever engage in activities which could be deemed harmful? If so, would you care to confess them to the rest of the group?

2. Do you think the author should have been using his time more wisely?

3. Do you think the author has any redeemable characteristics?

4. Would you care to know what happened next?

Aha, thought the hound, *it's Payday. Enough of them little chunks. Let's bring on the big stuff.*

As he took the bait, I hopped lightly onto his roof, then stood beside the doghouse, my ears plugged, my eyes shut tightly. My plan was falling into place flawlessly. I would wait for the muted explosions, wipe myself off, ring the doorbell, and calmly inform Mr. Henderson that his paper had arrived and that I was here to collect. Then I would add: "I think there's a problem with your dog."

But suddenly it dawned on me: I was the one with the problem. For one thing, there were no explosions. No howling. No flying fur. Evidently, the firecrackers were duds. To complicate matters, I had significantly overestimated Rancid's fondness for me. What first tipped me off was the velocity of his growl. And the fact that he was lunging toward me, fangs bared, fur vertical.

The tree branch was out of reach, so I charged the fence. In desperation, I threw my tiny body at the top of it, bounced hard, and landed chest first in Mr. Henderson's gladioli. For a moment I couldn't breathe. Then I heard it. A sweet sound. A wheezing sound.

Two feet away, Rancid had come to the end of his rope.

I wish I had learned an important lesson that evening. Something I could share with you to leave you just as breathless. But it would take a while. For the moment, all I could think of was, *I'll bet the soda-powered submarine is a dud, too.*

Just last Saturday, I flipped on the television and watched Frank Sinatra shuffle onto the stage and sing, "I did it my way . . ." and I thought to myself, *That's really sad, Frank. I hope you don't die singing that song.* Then I remembered: *That was my song, too.* That was my song in the gladioli patch. That's been my song through much of my life. Oh sure, I was a good Christian, so I didn't hum it too loudly. And I certainly didn't drive around with the bumper sticker "I love me and have a wonderful plan for my life." But that's the road I was traveling.

Perhaps you're like me. Perhaps you've spent your life mapping things out carefully, only to have them backfire. Or maybe you still believe that doing things your way will lead to the most exciting, most adventurous life of them all.

Let me tell you, it's a lie. When we pursue our own plans first, life will be a dud.

I remember preachers and missionaries telling us how they had found such joy in serving Jesus, and I would roll my eyes and think, *Oya, tell me about it. My name is Gertrude. I'll tell you a thing or two about adventure.* But in retrospect, I can see that they were right. I can see that life's greatest adventure didn't come in making a name for myself. It came when I began to follow the plans of Another. When I began to seek God.

Don't get me wrong. I still like to have loads of fun. Just ask my kids. But nothing holds a candle to the adventure of pursuing Jesus Christ with everything we've got. It's why we're here. When we make Him our plan, life will be an adventure book worth opening. An adventure book that will never end.

Study Guide Questions

Be Honest

1. Did you ever have a nickname? Was it nearly as bad as the author's?

2. Like the author, were you disappointed that the firecrackers didn't go off? What does this say about your overall character? About the author's overall character?

3. Was there a time in your life when you wanted to make a name for yourself? Is this still the case?

4. If you have children, what do you hope they will *do* when they get older? What do you hope they will *be?*

5. What would you say has been life's biggest adventure?

Go Deep

1. What do you think it means to "pursue Jesus Christ with everything we've got"?

2. Do you agree that "nothing holds a candle to the adventure of pursuing Jesus Christ with everything we've got"? Why or why not?

3. Read Psalm 34.

> *Taste and see that the LORD is good; blessed is the man who takes refuge in him. Fear the LORD, you his saints, for those who fear him lack nothing . . . those who seek the LORD lack no good thing.*
>
> **—Psalm 34:8-10**

CHAPTER NINE

What About Gord?

Cheerful company shortens the miles.

—German proverb

Gord Robideau and I first became acquainted in the corner of a hockey rink. In fact, he introduced himself to me with a hip-check I can still feel when the weather changes. As I groped about the ice, searching for the balance of my teeth, Gord skated toward the penalty box, dialoguing with the referee: "Aw, come on—" he said, but with more volume and less linguistic integrity, *"How could you tell I hit him? You don't even have your seeing-eye dog with you!"*

Partly to prove that I'm a forgiving sort, and partly because I admired his wit, I decided to get to know this guy.

So the next night I called him. No one was home except the answering machine. This is what it said:

> Hello, and welcome to the Mental Health Hotline. If you are obsessive-compulsive, please press 1 immediately. If you are codependent, please ask someone

else to press 2. If you have multiple personalities, please press 3, 4, 5, and 6. If you are paranoid, we know who you are and what you want. Just stay on the line so we can trace the call. If you are manic-depressive, it doesn't matter which number you press. No one will answer.

As you may have sensed by now, Gord needs a lot of help psychologically. Seriously, he's a fabulous guy. Except for one small problem: Gord watches a lot of baseball, so he scratches a lot. I mean a lot. If Gord misjudges a fly ball or duffs a tee shot, he will scratch his belly nonstop for the remainder of the day. I kid you not. He has worn out expensive wool sweaters this way. I tried to help him with the problem, but it's bigger than both of us.

During the past ten years, however, this has not hindered us from bonding like Super Glue. And, to be perfectly honest, Gord has helped me far more than I've helped him. For one thing, I can always think out loud around Gord. For another, whenever I made a fool of myself, he didn't think I'd done a permanent job. When I needed some good advice or a real corny joke, Gord was usually around. He would probably be scratching himself, but at least he was around. Gord was like a good tube of toothpaste—he always came through in a tight squeeze.

Last summer we climbed into an airplane, the toothpaste and I, and headed for our nation's capital where I was to speak. Gord loves politics, free food, and airline omelets, so when I assured him that I would pick up part of his airfare (about 11 dollars' worth), he was sold.

During the weekend we golfed, we ate, and when we got tired of that, we golfed. Gord kept reminding me that it's bad sportsmanship to pick up lost golf balls while they are still rolling. I think it appropriate to mention here that I beat him.[1]

"You know," I told him that night, as he sat on his side of the hotel room licking his wounds and scratching himself with the remote control, "I didn't bring you along for your looks."

"You're kidding," he said, flipping channels and laughing.

"Part of the reason is that I've just about had it with traveling."

Gord shut off the TV. "What do you mean?" he asked.

"I guess I always thought it would be loads of fun."

"It's not?"

"Well, it's better when a good friend is with you, but it ages fast. I guess I always glamorized travel. Thought it would mean new sights, eating out, peace and quiet. Mostly I've found it to be jam-packed with lonely people, long nights, and monstrous temptations. Take this TV, for instance. There are other channels on there besides the Disney channel, you know."

"You're kidding," he said, switching to his Dan Rather imitation: "Tonight we have 'Purple Passion in the Petunias.' Finally . . . a film with a plot!"

I went on to tell him of a trip to California. Of staying three blocks from Disneyland and walking down a plush hallway, when suddenly two semi-clad blonds who couldn't have been more than 18 stepped out of their room and into my

---

[1] To this day, Gord claims that I cheated. But I didn't. He alleges that I was using a Top Flite 1 and whenever I hit one into the rough, somehow miraculously I was able to find another just like it. He claims I had a special hole cut in my pocket and was releasing replacements down a pant leg. This is not true, and unfortunately, there are no replays available to aid my acquittal.

path. They asked me if I wanted to see their suite. I didn't think that's what they were after.

"What did you do?"

"I'm still not sure why I did it," I said, shaking my head and smiling.

"Did what?"

"Well, I started to run. And I didn't stop running until I was out of the hotel. The concierge thought I was nuts. I was laughing the whole way."

"You were? Alright! Waytago!" Gord lunged to his feet like we had just combined on an overtime goal. We slapped hands. "What were you laughing at?" he asked, sitting down.

"I'm still not sure. I guess I got to thinking how quickly a guy can mess up the rest of his life. And I was just glad I'd missed the opportunity."

For ten years Gord and I lived a block apart. We would walk his dog Saber together, then sit around the fire and confess our sins. I sincerely hope Saber isn't part parrot.

Recently, the two of them took Gord's wife, Joanne, and moved away, separating us by a mountain range and 500 miles. But Gord isn't the kind of guy you soon forget. Just before he left, I sat down to tell him so. I didn't verbalize my thoughts. Instead I picked up a pen and wrote a sensitive Nineties Guy Note, something he would cherish into old age:

Gord,

Just thought I'd drop you a note before you leave the Promised Land for sunnier pastures.

Thanks for your friendship over the years. There isn't anyone on earth I've enjoyed beating in sports (particularly golf, hockey, badminton, golf, Ping-Pong, checkers, chess, water polo, Monopoly, Parcheesi, and golf—just to name a few) more than you.

Seriously, my best memories are of the good talks we've had about everything under the sun. Other than your struggle with drooling, I have felt a real kinship. Seriously, my opinion of you grew greatly over the past few years when I watched you battle through some difficult decisions. I'm thankful for your commitment to Joanne and your love for her.

I wish you both all the best in your new home and trust that we will bump into each other on one of the long and winding roads of life as we near another land which is far better, and of course I speak here of retirement.

Seriously, you will be greatly missed.

Your friend, Phil

If you're a guy, I'm sure you understand why I was emotionally drained after writing this letter. You will also have noticed that I was forced to employ the word *seriously* on numerous occasions—sort of like I was pulling away from a hug.

Just for fun, let's contrast this letter with one I stole from my wife's Bible during church.[2] It was from her best friend Sherri, and it was written on flowered stationery, scented lightly with *Eau d' la Barge* perfume, and edited here for purposes of length and continuing peace in my marriage. Keep in mind that, unlike Gord, Ramona was not moving away.

---

[2] Not really. Be assured that I received the proper permission to reprint this here.

Ramona,

When you were away I thought of you often and I want you to know that I missed you. You are a gift from God and I value our friendship. I was thinking of the qualities that make you so special. Here are some of my thoughts:

- You love God and seek to do His will.

- You are a good mother. You love your kids. You're ready with smiles, hugs and words of encouragement when they need it. You nurture them physically, spiritually, and emotionally. You try to keep your eyes open so you can recognize when they need extra guidance and prayer.

- You are a loving wife. Even when frustrated with Phil[3] your love for him is evident. Your marriage is important to you.

- You are a good friend. You listen, you share yourself, you encourage when it's needed.

- You care deeply for others. You are sensitive and compassionate.

I feel blessed to have you for a friend. It's good to talk with you, laugh with you, and cry with you. We've gone through some difficult times, and we've tried to hold each other up—emotionally, spiritually, and sometimes even physically. We've spent time discussing God's Word, His will, and our heart's

---

[3] I still don't know why she said this.

desire to follow Him. I love you, dear friend, and I thank God for sending you into my life.

Love, Sherri

Guys like me aren't this good at sharing our feelings, but I think Gord understands. I think he knows that while he hasn't been nominated for sainthood yet, he has a friend for life.

Sometimes I wonder if he kept my note. Maybe it's in his top drawer. Maybe he pulls it out when he's down. And just for a minute, I'll bet he even stops scratching.

Study Guide Questions

Be Honest

1. Do you have a friend like Gord? If not, try to get one.
2. What are you doing to keep your friendships in good shape?
3. If you travel, is there someone (apart from God) to whom you're accountable? What can you do to make that happen?
4. How do you think you would respond to a "check out our suite" situation?

Go Deep

1. Read the story of Joseph in Genesis 39 or rent and watch the video "Joseph" (starring Ben Kingsley and Martin Landau). Think over question four (above) again.

2. At a time when so many people are moving around the country, those who don't make new acquaintances find themselves alone. What are some things you could do to make new friends? Are you building walls or bridges?

3. Read Proverbs 16:28; 17:17; 18:24; 27:6.

4. Henry Ward Beecher said, "Do not keep the alabaster boxes of your love and tenderness sealed up until your friends are dead." Are there some things you've left unsaid?

5. Write a friend this week. See how many times you can use the word "seriously."

Friendship is one of the sweetest joys of life. Many might have failed beneath the bitterness of their trial had they not found a friend.

—Charles Haddon Spurgeon (1834–1892)

CHAPTER TEN

Men and Women: Exploring the Difference

You never know the best about men until you know the worst about them.

—G.K. Chesterton

In this chapter I intend to trace in great detail the historical roots of the masculine and feminine identities, exploring at great length our conflicting drives and complex desires, bringing us at last to a definitive understanding of the fact that while cataclysmic differences so easily separate men and women, they can also engender mutual respect and a better understanding of why God made us distinct creatures.

On second thought, maybe I'll just do up some charts and graphs which we'll find way more interesting.

Are Boys and Girls Different?

In answering this question, I think it's important to realize two things:

a. There are no bad questions.

b. This one comes real close.

91

A recent ground-breaking study concludes that while the two genders may live under the same roof, they rarely reside under the same ozone layer. I was able to save a fair amount of cash by conducting the study myself this past Saturday. The results are documented below.

(Please bear in mind that this survey was drawn from a random sampling of three kids that were hanging around our house at the time. When considering the responses of this many children, we can be 33 percent confident that the conclusions are accurate to within 66 percentage points and 95 percent confident that by the time the results were compiled, the pollster was 100 percent exhausted and should not be held responsible for glaring errors.)

Boys' and Girls' Activity Comparison Chart

Typical Saturday Morning

Time*	Rachael	Stephen and Jeffrey
6:30	Sleeping soundly, one arm around favorite doll	Gearing up for a new day by pounding on each other
8:04	Eating Breakfast	Throwing Breakfast
8:26	Getting dressed for the thirteenth time	Pounding on each other
9:17	Locating coloring books	Locating sticks, rocks, assorted weapons
10:11	Phoning friends	Poking friends
11:30	Riding bike	Trying to make bikes sound louder
11:43	Pretending to make dinner	Looking for dinner

*All times are Mountain Standard.

Men and Women: Exploring the Difference

Back when I had tons of child-rearing theories and no actual children, I would have frowned on this chart. I would have considered writing the author an unsigned note myself, and maybe enclosing something explosive. But today, I am thoroughly convinced that if you took a group of little boys and a group of little girls, and somehow you found willing parties who would raise them responsibly on separate planets—without He–Man action figures, without dolls—that the girls would somehow find a way to build homes and nurture one another, while the boys (if they didn't strangle each other first) would invent guns and possibly space ships to visit the girls' planet and chase them around, yelling.[1]

Sure, you may be thinking, boys and girls are different. But over the last few decades there has been much progress in bridging the gap between men and women. Besides, didn't they look real similar during the '70s?

Perhaps the following chart will lead to meaningful discussion, increased sensitivity, and greater understanding as we seek to explore the answers to this complex question. Then again, it might just make people really mad and lead to greater hostility.[2]

Adult Activity Chart

A table containing blatant generalizations

Stimulus	Female Response	Male Response
Weddings	Plan for them, talk about them, reminisce about them, cry at them	Avoid them

[1] This is a hypothetical situation. I am not recommending that you enlist your children in any such program.

[2] I admit that much of my own experience has been worked into this chart, but I hope you will be able to identify. I hope you will recognize someone here. I hope you will smile and nod your head before pounding on them.

Stimulus	Female Response	Male Response
Sports	Enjoy figure skating, gymnastics	Enjoy full-contact gymnastics
Cats	Cuddle them	Chase them
Plants	Water them, nurture them	Kill them
School	Time of growth, education, sociological development	Spitwads
Bathrooms	Decorate them	Mess them
Mistakes	Occasionally admit them	We definitely have a problem here. In fact, the last guy to admit he was wrong was General George Custer, and you know what happened to him.
Laundry	Once or twice a week.	Laundry? What's a laundry?
Romance	Ah, it makes the world go round	Once or twice a week

The Way We Are

If you are married or find yourself considering the option, allow me to offer you a little advice. It's not the most profound thing you'll ever lay eyes on, but I believe it is an important foundational truth:

God made men and women different.

And it's okay. In fact, it's great.

Because of God's grace, we can come to the point where we enjoy those differences—even celebrate them. We can come to the point where we say, "Hey, that's the way he is. And it's okay. In fact, I'm not going to pound on him. I'm not going to send him nasty letters. I won't even enclose explosives."

Now, I'd better go. The boys are looking for supper.

Study Guide Questions

Be Honest

1. Did anything in this chapter upset you? Did you read anything to your spouse?

2. Do you agree that "God made men and women distinct creatures"?

3. What are some ways your spouse is different from you? Does this sometimes drive you nuts?

4. Socrates said, "By all means, marry. If you get a good wife, you will become very happy. If you get a bad one, you will become a philosopher." Do you think enjoying your differences will help keep you from becoming a philosopher?

Go Deep

1. In his book *Men and Women*, Larry Crabb wrote, "Occasionally the immature bliss of honeymoon love yields to a growing relationship between people who notice their own flaws more than those of their mates, who are troubled more by their own selfishness than by that of their spouse, and who make it a priority to become better companions. These become the truly great marriages, and they are rare." How rare is your marriage?

2. Have you realized yet how badly and how often you need forgiveness?

3. Read Larry Crabb's book *Men and Women* (Zondervan Publishing House).

4. Read Philippians 2:1-18.

5. Take your spouse out for dinner. Talk about your differences—then celebrate them.

A happy marriage is the union of two good forgivers.
—Robert Quillen (1887–1948)

CHAPTER ELEVEN

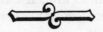

The Trouble with Brandi

A silly idea is current that good people do not know what temptation means. This is an obvious lie. Only those who try to resist temptation know how strong it is. . . . We never find out the strength of the evil impulse inside us until we try to fight it: and Christ, because He was the only man who never yielded to temptation, is also the only man who knows to the full extent what temptation means—the only complete realist.

—C.S. Lewis

At the ripe old age of ten, while riding my brother's Golden Hawk three-speed, I ran over a naked woman. Squeaking to a halt, I hopped off the bicycle, and ran back to see if she was okay. She looked alright to me—despite the painful tire tracks—but just to make sure, I bent over, picked her up, and discovered that she folded in half right around the hips.

Amazing, I thought.

Her name was Brandi, and, if I recall correctly, her last name didn't make much sense because it consisted solely of hyphenated numbers.

It is tough to describe the feeling that came over me as I tried to remove the tire tracks from her body, so I won't even try. But holding her that day I realized I had a problem. I couldn't just leave her there, cold and abandoned, but what to do? Surely my mother would not approve if I brought Brandi home. After all, we did not dress like this at our house. We dressed decently and in order.

So, tucking her beneath my coat, I climbed aboard the Golden Hawk and carried her past smiling neighbors to my fort in the woods. There I located an old newspaper, wrapped Brandi up tightly, and buried her in a solemn ceremony two trees down from the fort.

I think I forgot about her then—until the day Puberty arrived on my doorstep, knocked loudly, and requested that I return to the woods and search for her remains.

Looking back, I'm glad I was unable to find them, but I must confess there were times when I wasn't so pleased; times when I cruised around our small town on the Golden Hawk hoping to run over some of her friends.

Last summer, my friend Vance and I, together with our wives, sat on a beach, admiring the landscape. The sun was warm; the sand was hot; the surf was up. *Ah, it doesn't get any better than this,* I thought. Ramona was entertaining seagulls with McDonald's french fries. The rest of us were busy spreading sun tan lotion.

"Isn't it beautiful?" said Ramona, gazing out to sea.

At this point, a girl, who had not spent a great deal on the material for her costume, walked by. Momentarily, we guys forgot about the seagulls.

"Yes, it sure is beautiful," I observed, before being pelted with french fries.

Vance concurred wholeheartedly. "Boy, did God know what He was doing when He knocked out Adam," he said. Ironically, Vance was clubbed hard on the side of the head right then. With a snorkel.

"It's true," I said, tossing french fries to the birds. "As sure as God made seagulls, He made women. And I think it's pretty clear which one He spent the most time on."

Vance was still shaking off the blow. "Ladies," he wheezed, "guys can't help but notice these things. If we didn't notice these things the human race would have gone the way of the Great Fluorescent Owl. We were simply appreciating God's design. It's possible to notice a beautiful woman without lusting after her. We're not following her down the beach. . . . yow, my head hurts too much to move anyway!"

We assured our wives of our undying devotion to them. Vance quoted portions of Song of Solomon. And I reclined on my purple beach towel, wondering where I could get Ramona one of those little costumes.

Steve knows all about costumes and cruising on three-speeds.

I was speaking at a church recently. Afterwards, a man about my age came forward. He held a leather briefcase in his right hand and in his left a matching jacket. As I finished talking with some others, he stood to one side, waiting. When they were gone, he approached me. "Hi," I said. Transferring the briefcase, he shook my hand and introduced himself. His name was Steve and when I asked how he was doing, he was honest: "Not very good."

"I'm sorry," I said. "You want to tell me about it?"

Silence.

"Let me take a few guesses. If I don't get it right then you have to help me." For the first time he looked me in the eye and cracked a smile.

"Is it . . . substance abuse?"

He paused, glancing around the room nervously. "Sort of."

"Drugs?"

"No."

"An addiction?"

"Yah. Definitely."

"Pornography?"

"Yes. . . . How did you nail it so quickly?"

"Because 90 percent of Christian guys today struggle at some time with it."

"What about the others?"

"Well," I said, "six percent are pathological liars and the other four have a medical problem."

We laughed, then sat down on the steps of the church platform. I told him about the day I met Brandi, and that I'd run over a few of her friends along the road, too. He told me about the videotapes, about the magazines. "I don't know how many I've burned over the years," he confessed. "But I keep going back. I thought it would get easier when I got married. Then I thought it would get easier as I got older. Turns out it's the opposite."

We sat in silence.

"You know," I said, "the battle isn't over for me either. Two months ago I was hooked up to the Internet. You can now sit in the privacy of an office, press five or six computer keys, wait a few minutes, and come face to face with the most explicit pictures ever available. And no one has to know. Like all technology, the Internet makes a useful servant but a lousy master. It can leave you feeling like you've run over a truckload of magazines. And you can't just bury the problem."

"What do you do about it?"

"Well, the first thing I did was paste a verse right above the screen on my monitor: 'Teach us how short our lives really are so that we may be wise.'[1] I've found that when God's Word is running through my veins I'm less likely to indulge the flesh."

"What else?" he asked.

"I hope this doesn't sound trite," I said, "but the Internet has made me realize how badly I need God. It has helped me discover that the closer I walk with Him, the more I meditate on His Word and the more I don't want to put anything between us. You see, pornography kills relationships. It alienates us from our spouses. Our kids. From God."

"Boy, you're not kidding." There was more silence.

"I think you need to be encouraged that you're struggling, Steve," I said.

"I should?"

I tried to remember an Oswald Chambers quote I had heard, something like, "The sign that the Holy Spirit is working in me is not that I don't have sinful desires, it is that I am not dominated by them."

"But that's me," he said. "Dominated."

"Have you told any friends about it?" I asked.

"No," he replied. "I don't know anyone like that."

I encouraged him to get to know other guys in his church, and to be honest with them. But he wouldn't say much more. Picking up his briefcase, he stood to leave. "Write me," I said, handing him my card. "I'll pray for you."

That was the last time I heard from Steve.

Not long ago I was talking to Gordon MacDonald, author of *Ordering Your Private World.* Ten years ago, due to a moral

---

[1] Psalm 90:12, New Century Version.

failure, Gordon's private world fell apart. When I asked him about it, he gave me some advice I've never forgotten. "Evangelicalism in America has bought into the culture of individualism," he said. "Each of us is a solo performer. We have books, conferences and seminars telling individuals how to survive and thrive. But what helps people survive and thrive is not information. It's the accountability, support, and rebuke that comes from being in a tightly knit group. I need men in my life who will look me square in the eye and say, 'Gordon, at this point you're full of it. If I had that kind of friend ten years ago, we wouldn't be talking about failure today.'"

Sometimes I think about Steve. And I pray for him.

I pray that he'll stick close to a friend named Jesus. A friend of sinners like Steve. And sinners like me. A friend who said, "My grace is sufficient for you, for my power is made perfect in weakness."[2]

And I pray that he'll find a friend like Vance. A friend who freely admits he's ridden a few bicycles himself. That he's hit a few speed bumps along the way. And although he's still shaking off a snorkel blow to the head, he has enough sense left to know that we ride a dangerous road when we travel it alone.

Study Guide Questions

Be Honest

1. Can you remember the first time you "ran over a naked woman"? What was your reaction?

[2] 2 Corinthians 12:9.

2. After I spoke at a men's retreat, someone told me they never go swimming because they can't deal with the temptations around them. Is this the right response for you? What do you think of the statement, "It's possible to notice a beautiful woman without lusting after her"?

3. To what extent do you struggle with pornography?

   ☐ greatly   ☐ too much   ☐ somewhat   ☐ very little

4. Chicago White Sox co-owner Jerry Reinsdorf once said, "I know how to tell when George Steinbrenner is lying. His lips move." Accountability requires honesty. Are you being truthful in your relationships? Do you have a friend like Vance? What would it take to find one?

Go Deep

1. Do you agree that pornography kills relationships? Alienates us from our spouses? Our kids? From God? If so, how important is it that we eliminate it from our lives? What has helped you the most in this battle?

2. Are you hooked up to the Internet? Do you need to be? If not, unhook. Otherwise, tell a trusted Christian friend of any problems. Seek ways to block access to explicit material.

3. Is your hero one who rides into town with nothing but a six-shooter, straightens things out, and rides off into the sunset by himself? Do Gordon MacDonald's words describe you? In what ways have you bought into "the culture of individualism"?

4. Patrick Morley says, "There is power in vulnerability, strength in numbers, and safety in visibility." Are you in an accountability group? If not, are you ready for one? What's the next step?

5. Are you living in daily awareness of your weaknesses? Where do you go when you fail?

6. Answer the following questions honestly: Are you a man after God's own heart? Are you willing to follow Him no matter what the cost? When you fall, do you get on your knees with your Bible, then get back up? Read Psalm 51.

God wants to develop the same character traits in us as exist in Christ. We are to react to the situations of life as Christ did.

—Erwin W. Lutzer

CHAPTER TWELVE

A Funny Thing Happened on the Way to the Monastery

I am an optimist. It does not seem too much use being anything else.

—Winston Churchill

I was a very intelligent child in grade two. So intelligent that low marks did not discourage me at all. I read two picture books a week, knew how to count quarters, and could speak quite eloquently on a variety of topics—even when asked not to.

Mrs. MacLaren must have recognized my extraordinary potential because two or three times a week she requested that I stay after school and work on it. I think she appreciated my handwriting also, because sometimes she would have me fill the whole blackboard with it: "I will naut shoot spitwods I will lissen better toomorow."

Then we would work on my spelling.

Afterward, I got to put my head on my desk and close my eyes for a full 15 minutes. This was kind of Mrs. MacLaren because by that time, I needed the rest.

Sometimes, I must admit, I peeked. And when I did, I could see her sitting at her wooden desk shuffling papers and sipping black coffee from a silver thermos. By quitting time each day, she had far exceeded the recommended dosage, and when my 15 minutes were up, she had no trouble summoning the strength to motion me forward. I stood still before her, listening as she shared some observations.

"Philip," she would intone, thrusting each syllable toward me, "when will you learn that putting Elmer's Glue on little girls' pigtails is no way for a boy to behave?"[1] Then she would offer me a butterscotch mint.

I liked those mints, and I liked Mrs. MacLaren. But let's be honest here. This did not make up for the fact that you could smell her breath in South America.

To this day I can't stand coffee.[2]

Confessions of a Hopeful Romantic

I did, however, become addicted to other things. Baseball. Marbles. Even fairy-tale books. Sometimes, when there was a break in my schedule, I would sit, twirling my hair with one hand and leafing through fairy-tale books with the other. *Peter Pan, The Ugly Duckling, Snow White.* I liked the pictures, and

---

[1] In later years, I learned that she suffered from migraine headaches. I believe there are several possible explanations. Here are just a few:

    a. Caffeine.

    b. Me.

[2] Historical note: In the eighteenth century, King Gustav III of Sweden, convinced that coffee was a poison, sentenced a murderer to death by the drinking of one cup a day. In the interests of science, he provided a comparison group for his experiment—another murderer, whom he pardoned on the proviso that he would drink one cup of tea daily. Since doctors know when someone is deceased, King Gustav appointed two physicians to follow the cases. The results are fascinating: First, the doctors died; followed by King Gustav, who was murdered; and the tea drinker, who succumbed at the age of 83. The coffee drinker outlived them all. I still do not like coffee.

especially the happily-ever-after part. It appealed to my optimistic outlook, my sanguine soul.

One day, after reading *Snow White*, I became so optimistic that I began looking for princesses. *Maybe I'll kiss one*, I thought, *and see if she wakes up.*

Joy King sat across from me for most of that year. Her dimples were the size of nine-iron divots, and she framed them quite nicely in golden-blond hair. Until those dimples, I hadn't much use for girls. They pinched harder than boys, and they screamed louder, too. But one day after spelling class, Mrs. MacLaren had Joy and me share a solitary desk to check each other's work for errors. I found nothing but perfection on her list, and I checked it very thoroughly, indeed.

As if the dimples weren't enough, Joy wore soft-knit pastel sweaters, and she played the violin beautifully. I felt called to take up the instrument myself that day, but despite weeks of practice, I couldn't make the strings do the things Joy could, and nobody wanted me in their orchestra. In a last-ditch effort to impress her, I followed her home from school one day and somehow mustered up enough courage to throw snowballs at her golden head. Sometimes, when I hear a violin solo, I wonder what happened to Joy King.

Faded Dreams

By the time fourth grade rolled around, the memory of Joy was beginning to fade. Three seats ahead of me Gloryanne Larue's raven-black hair cascaded toward her white blouse and into my life. She wore black penny loafers, tartan knee socks, and a smile that could light up your entire solar system if you let it.

On Valentine's Day, 1971, that smile got the best of me, and I rose to my feet, walked past it, and placed a wad of fresh chewing gum in the wastebasket. On the journey back, I casually eased a shiny Canadian dime onto Gloryanne's desktop, knowing that, although my magnetic personality was enough of a draw, this small offering would undoubtedly seal our relationship, binding us together for time and eternity.

I was wrong.

Instead, she seized the dime and never looked back.

For days afterward I sat behind the raven, regretting my decision, knowing that I could have bought two bags of Valentine hearts, found a quiet place, and eaten them myself.

I also wanted the gum back.

Later that year Ruthie Pike helped me forget my bad investment when she took my hand on a skating rink. I have written about the event in chapter 2 and it is too painful to recount the details once again. Allow me to say, however, that the following Monday during mathematics, I inscribed her initials in huge letters on both sides of my binder: R.P. I also did so on my jeans.

The next summer Ruthie moved away, leaving only her initials behind. The jeans even faded.

In grade five I took a liking to Rachel Peterson for a while, and once again displayed the binder proudly. She dumped me like brussels sprouts once her boyfriend found out, and the only R.P. left in the whole school was a short little freckled kid by the name of Rodney Perkins. I ditched the binder that day. And seriously considered spending the rest of my life in a monastery, devoted to silence.

Coming to Life

I could go on and on about girls, but I think we're all depressed enough. The simple, painful truth is this: They never went on and on about me.

Can you identify?

Be honest. Wasn't there a time in your life when you wanted to ditch the binder? Wasn't there a time when it dawned on you: Fairy tales don't come to life?

Everywhere I go I meet guys who have watched relationships fizzle and fall through the grate. If that's where you find yourself today, let me offer a ray of hope to light up your solar system: There is One who will never leave you, never forsake you. He's the only One who knows exactly where you've been and where you're going. And He loves you just the same.

In a note I received from my friend Max Lucado, he wrote,

> God's love never ceases. Never. Though we spurn Him. Ignore Him. Reject Him. Despise Him. Disobey Him. He will not change. Our evil cannot diminish His love. Our goodness cannot increase it. Our faith does not earn it any more than our stupidity jeopardizes it. God doesn't love me less if I fail. He doesn't love me more if I succeed. God's love never ceases.

Maybe fairy tales come to life after all.

Study Guide Questions

Be Honest

1. Can you remember something good about your second-grade teacher?

2. Can you name something that's been a major disappointment?

3. Can you remember the first love of your life? How old were you? How long did it last?

4. Did you ever give a girl something you wish you could have back?

5. Did you ever consider taking up residence in a monastery?

Go Deep

1. Tony Campolo said, "God carries your picture in His wallet." Do you have trouble seeing God this way? Why or why not?

2. Read the book of 1 John (it will take 7 or 8 minutes).

3. Read Max Lucado's book *No Wonder They Call Him the Savior* (Multnomah).

Christian love, either toward God or toward man, is an affair of the will. But the great thing to remember is that, though our feelings come and go, his love for us does not.

—C. S. Lewis

CHAPTER THIRTEEN

The Girl Next Door

We waste time looking for the perfect lover, instead of creating the perfect love.

—Tim Robbins

Those years in the monastery were not easy ones. The robes. The walls. The thick silence. I found an old radio once and thought I'd found company. But the stone walls made good reception impossible. I turned up the volume and only got static.

Loneliness ate at my soul like those South American fish that can strip you to the bone in 60 seconds flat. We were only allowed to say two words every two years in the monastery, and when I got my chance, I told the others: "Food cruddy." Two years later I said: "Bed lumpy."

On the night of my fifteenth birthday, I sat alone on that bed, looking out at the stars, quietly strumming my ukulele, and humming sorrowful tunes to comfort my heart.

The very next day I stood during breakfast and told the other monks I'd had enough. "I'm outta here," I said, far exceeding my word limit. Then I smashed the ukulele over my porridge bowl for emphasis. They told me they didn't care. All I ever did was complain anyway.

On a cloudless August evening in grade ten, I stopped complaining. Standing in a small circle of friends, listening to Stephen Rendall describe the latest edition of a Buick Riviera, my mouth dropped open. "Who's that?" I interrupted, turning owl-like to watch her pass.

"Oh, that's the new girl," said Stephen, "Bjorn or something. . . . So the mag wheels are totally chrome and you should see the dash . . . "

There are times in life when cars don't move you like they used to—times when you know the monastery is out of the question, and you think again of fairy tales and dream that you will one day play a leading role.

The leading lady sat two desks ahead of me for English 10. Observers didn't require much schooling to realize we were not in the same class, though. Her name was Ramona Bjorndal, and she was beautiful. No, let's be accurate: She was gorgeous. Fair-skinned. Exquisite. All decked out in regal splendor. I was, well . . . I was none of the above. Someone else would undoubtedly woo her. Someone with charm. Pizzazz. Cash. I was a wounded optimist. All I had going for me was hope.

Two weeks after school began, however, that hope paid off. Two weeks after school began, she moved in next door.

Watching through the dryer vent in our laundry room, I cracked my knuckles and smiled. It was just a matter of time before I won her hand.

The ensuing months saw a marked improvement in my devotional life. For one thing, I memorized verses. Verses like, "Love thy neighbor as thyself."[1] I also began to pray with greater urgency. I prayed she would notice me, and that she would like what she noticed. I prayed she would see that true

---

[1] I wasn't so concerned with context in those days.

contentment lies not in getting what you thought you wanted, but in liking what you get.

One Friday evening, while outside pretending to weed Mom's flower garden in the pouring rain, I watched Ramona step outside and unfurl her umbrella. We exchanged glances over a hedge.

"Hi," I said nervously, "how are you doing?"

"Fine," she said wistfully, " . . . except my cat is missing."

Now, I had never been real fond of cats.[2] In fact, for years I maintained that if you took all the cats on the earth and lined them up end to end on the surface of the moon, you would be a lot better off. But that night, after scouring the neighborhood with Ramona and finding no cats, I started to like them.[3]

We stood under the umbrella together, Ramona and I, watching dismal gray clouds turn pearl pink, then fiery red. We spoke of pets, of English class, of weather. And as the sun broke through the clouds to soften her oval face, I popped the question: "I'm hoping to get my driver's license soon. Would you like to go bowling?"

She popped the umbrella. And told me she would.

---

[2] Cats, I believed, were at best couch ornaments. They did not need people and, furthermore, they had an air of condescension. C.S. Lewis seemed to agree. He once wrote in a letter, "We were talking about cats and dogs the other day and decided that both have consciences but the dog, being an honest, humble person, always has a bad one, but the cat is a Pharisee and always has a good one. When he sits and stares you out of countenance he is thanking God that he is not as these dogs, or these humans, or even as these other cats!"

[3] We never did find the cat, although one report claimed that it had climbed up into a car engine and not come out. At least, not the way it went in.

The First Miss

"So, have you, like, *kissed her yet?*" We'd been dating for more than a year, and friends were beginning to question my hormonal proficiency.

"No," I answered. "I haven't *kissed her yet.*"

"Ha, ha, ha," they responded. "You dweeb."

I wanted to explain that love had taught me some painful lessons, and that this time I would take it slow. Instead, I said, "When I do kiss her, it won't be because two guys *who don't even have their own girlfriends* told me to."

"Ooh," they snickered. "Take it easy. It's no big deal."

But it was a big deal for me.

One night, as we sat in Dad's driveway, the moon rising before us and Olivia Newton John breathing heavily through 100-watt speakers, I knew the time had come. Reaching over, I took her hand, puckered my lips . . . and chickened out.

"Well," I said softly, still holding her hand, "I guess I'd better be going."

"Pardon me?"

I turned down the stereo.

"Um . . . thanks for bowling with me, Ramona. Let's try something else next time."

"Okay."

"Um . . . I guess I'd better be going then."

"Okay."

Silence.

"Good night."

"Good night."

I could hear the voices of my friends. And the beating of my heart. And Olivia crooning. "I love you . . . I honestly love you. . . ."[4] So I moistened my lips, leaned over, and landed a poor excuse for a kiss squarely on the left half of her smile.

---

[4] I was in love with Olivia Newton John once for a week or so, but then, who wasn't?

Then I opened the door and marched awkwardly into the house.

It was over.

After 57 weeks and three days, it was over. The fat lady had sung. The last dog had been hung. The cows had come home. After all, he who kisses like a frog wakes only himself. I would go back to studying cars. Maybe check out another monastery.

But love has a way of surprising us sometimes, doesn't it? With a little hindsight, I could have looked back at the car that night and seen Ramona sitting there. She was a little dazed. But she was smiling.

And the very next evening she pursed her lips and asked me to try again.

Happily Ever After?

Five years later, on August 28, 1982, we joined hands and nervously said, "I do." It was a wild promise made before God and several hundred witnesses. And I kissed her that day. I kissed her like never before.

At the time, I thoroughly believed that fairy tales come true. I thoroughly believed that, with a few rare exceptions, we would waltz off into the sunset and close the book. Call me naive, but I had no idea she would leave taps on, slam cupboard doors, and remain deathly silent while I tried to have a good argument. She had no idea she was marrying a stubborn sportaholic. One who would demand more at times than she could deliver. One who would create more messes than he would clean.

To be honest, neither of us knew the years ahead would throw us some curveballs even a die-hard optimist wouldn't know how to hit. Without giving you an organ recital, allow me to say that the last four years have been less than ideal. In fact, they've been the most difficult of my life. The one I waltz with has been dancing very little. We've seen more doctors, more specialists, and more hospital wards, and more ambulances than you ever want to see. And as I write, we are staring down the barrel of an uncertain future. They don't warn you of this in the fairy-tale books.

But there are a few things that remain crystal clear. Whatever happens, I will stick by this girl. Whatever happens, I will follow the only One who promises a happily-ever-after—and really delivers. Take it from me. A hopeless romantic who turned into an eternal optimist.

Study Guide Questions

Be Honest

1. Think way back to your first kiss. Did you do better than the author? Have you had a second opinion on this?

2. If you are married, do you remember the first time you saw your wife to be? What impression did you have?

3. Like the author, did you pursue your wife until she caught you? Who chased whom?

4. Were you under any outside pressure to become involved physically? Were you under any inside pressure? What happened?

Go Deep

1. What surprises awaited you in the first few years of marriage?

2. Have the years thrown you some curve-balls? How have you handled them?

3. Singer Roberta Flack said, "Getting married is easy. Staying married is more difficult. Staying happily married for a lifetime should rank among the fine arts." Do you agree? How

committed are you to staying happily married for a life-time—no matter what comes your way?

4. With your spouse read *The Mystery of Marriage* (Multnomah) by Mike Mason.

5. Read *When Life Doesn't Turn Out Like You Planned* (Nelson Publishers) by Bill Butterworth.

We have a God who loves. That means that we have a God who suffers.

—J. B. Phillips

CHAPTER FOURTEEN

Of Toes and Tongues

Preach the gospel all the time; if necessary use words.

—St. Francis of Assisi

Crazy things happen when you're a parent. Even crazier things when you're a crazy parent.

On Wednesday night I hit the "Power On" button on our remote control. As I suspected, it powered up the television. I had no idea it would power up the kids. But, sure enough, three seconds later they were rolling on the floor in great fits of laughter.

On-screen a man approximately six times the width of their father was singing his way through an opera as if it were the last thing he would ever be allowed to do. Great beads of sweat plunged down his face. Great rounds of applause greeted his every inflection. Stephen, Rachael, and Jeffrey had never seen anything like it. He was hitting notes they never knew existed, in a language they hadn't heard before. This was shaping up to be more exciting than the Christmas pageant in which

Mrs. Goertzen's wig slipped slowly from her head during her solo rendition of "O Little Town of Bethlehem."

Watching the big guy holler, I thought of a statement I'd heard somewhere: "An opera is where the leading lady gets stabbed and instead of dying, she sings."

"Do you know why he's singing like that?" I asked, for a reason I still can't recall. The children turned from the screen, wiped their eyes, and tried hard to listen. "Because," I said, "someone put a pin in his seat."

This did not lessen the hilarity of the moment, and I seized the opportunity, slid onto the carpet, and started tickling them.

The next day at work, the phone called. I answered. It was my wife. "Honey, there's a bit of a problem at school." Now, if the purpose of an opening line is to get your attention, this one has to rank right up there with, "Hey, Mrs. Wittman, there's a snake in your blouse."

A problem at school.

"Uh . . . this won't be good news then?" I asked.

"See what you think," she replied.

"Stephen had choir today," she began. "You know, Stephen, *your* eldest son?" I don't know why she said this. Perhaps she hoped to bring a little humor to the situation. "I'm not sure what the song was," she continued, "but suddenly he began to sing way louder than normal. Way higher than normal. With lots of warble." *Uh oh.* My mind was racing on ahead of her.

"Everyone decided to stop singing so they could watch Stephen. The teacher too. Finally she stopped his brief and unwelcome solo debut with, *'Hey, cut it out right now.'* Then she asked, 'Stephen, what are you doing?'

"'Singing,' he said, 'opera.'"

"'Why,' she asked, 'are you doing that?'

"'Because,' he replied, 'someone put a pin in my seat.'"
Apparently the rest of the practice didn't go so smoothly.

I sat in my office, trying to think positively: *Hey, it's nice to know this generation can hear our words above the music.*

Then I thought of the day I learned what speaks loudest of all.

Shpeed

I'm not a big man poundage-wise, but when I sing, I sound bigger. Just ask my boys. As I mentioned, we have two of them. They were born of the same parents. Born in the same hospital room. But I have to tell you, these guys are from different planets.

You can see it clearly on Saturdays. Stephen sits on the sidewalk, observing ants. Tenderly he feeds them sugar and bread crumbs. Nurturing their faithful habits. Their every wish his command. "Daddy," asks our biologist son, "did you realize that the total weight of all the ants in the world is greater than that of the humans?" I did not know this, and I'm reluctant to admit it to an eight-year-old.

Thankfully, Jeffrey arrives to rescue me. He is bedecked in camouflage pants. Army hat. Black boots. Assorted sticks. A five-year-old dressed to kill.

Striding through the ant colony, he obliterates the population in seconds, grinning at the soft crunching sound, scoring points for the humans. Stephen, the pacifist, turns very active then. There is screaming. And Jeffrey runs like the wind.

Now, normally the boy does not move this fast. Normally he moves about as swiftly as a bill through Congress. Take Sunday mornings, for instance. If they posted a "Last One into the Sanctuary" listing on the church bulletin board, Jeffrey would come in second (his mother would be singled out for top honors, but that's another chapter). Yes, during the time it takes him to locate his socks, the rest of us can watch *Ben Hur, The Ten Commandments,* and *The Sound of Music,* pausing often for refreshments and a round or two of Monopoly. But the moment Jeffrey steps into the car, he undergoes an amazing transformation. "Go, Daddy, go," he chants. "Go, Daddy, go."

Stephen, the biologist, is horrified. "Don't speed," he scolds, both eyes on the speedometer. "We're not allowed to speed."

It is good advice, the benefits of which can be measured far beyond good gas mileage. Parents who obey the laws of the land model respect. Responsibility. Obedience. "A good example is the best sermon," I've always said. "You can preach a better sermon with your toes than with your tongue." And so I keep one eye on the speedometer at all times. Or at least I *did*.

Until today.

Today, Jeffrey and I are traveling to a nearby city where I will speak to a church group. I like bringing the kids when I travel. It's an ideal opportunity for us to spend some quantity time together. Besides, if my message gets dull, I can use them for illustrations.

"Daddy," says Jeffrey, "I'm glad I'm with just you."

"Ah, thanks, Jeff," I reply, breaking open a package of gum and handing him a piece. "I'm glad, too."

"'Cuz," he continues, "'cuz Rachael and Stephen can't boss me."

"Do they boss you lots?"

"Ya, but not today. Today I'll be boss, okay?"

"Sure," I say, wondering where I left my good judgment.

"Dad, you say 'no' lots." Jeffrey is pushing his luck.

"Well, I'll tell you what. I'll try to say 'yes' all day."

The child smiles, then takes the package of gum. Smiling wider still, he pops another stick into his mouth. Then another.

"Jeffrey—"

"You said you wouldn't say 'no.'"

Moments later he has inserted *the whole pack*, but somehow he manages: "Go *fashter*, Dad. Go s*hpeed*."

"Jeffrey," I say, realizing an important teaching time has arisen, "there will always be someone to obey. No matter how big you get, you'll have to listen to someone."

He peers out the window, his newfound freedom undaunted. The prairie grass sways in the wind. Telephone poles whiz by like fence posts. For, you see, his father is running a little late. His father has taken an eye off the speedometer. Whereas, moments ago, he was singing "God Will Take Care of You," now, as the speedometer touches 60, he is humming "Guide Me, O Thou Great Jehovah." At 65, it's "Nearer, My God, to Thee." At 75, "Nearer, Still Nearer." At 85, he breaks into a medley of songs: "This World Is Not My Home," "Take Me Home Country Roads," and finally, "Precious Memories."

Suddenly, the humming turns to a low whistle. The child is enjoying the colorful light show in the side mirror. The father is not. Rolling down my window, I hear a tall man in a blue cap ask, "Was there a nuclear attack?"

"No . . . heh, heh . . . I am . . . well . . . guilty, Officer. One hundred percent." The officer is temporarily speechless.

Seventy-two dollars later, so am I.

"Who was that guy?" asks Jeffrey.

"That was one of the guys I have to obey."

"Did ya obey him?"

"No. But I'm going to do a little better from now on."

As we pull slowly away, my mind goes to the sermon I'm about to preach. I will touch on important concepts like integrity, faithfulness, and obedience. And a little boy will listen. Yet what he hears won't hold a candle to what he sees.

For now, Jeffrey sits quietly, blowing bubbles, listening to the skinny guy whistle, and wondering how he'll explain our little adventure to his big brother.

Study Guide Questions

Be Honest

1. Have you ever said anything really crazy to your kids? What did you do about it?

2. Do you own a radar detector? Why or why not?

3. *Robin:* "Batgirl! What took you so long?"
   Batgirl: "You wouldn't believe the traffic, and the lights were all against me. Besides, you wouldn't want me to speed, would you?"
   Robin: "Your good driving habits almost cost us our lives!"
   Batman: "No, Robin, she's right. Rules are rules."
   Who do you most agree with?

4. What kind of driver are you? How heavy is your foot? Do you drive differently when you are alone? Why or why not?

5. Do you think cruise control was a good invention? By whose standard do you set it?

6. Do you think the remote control was a good invention? By whose standard do you set it?

Go Deep

1. Mark Twain said, "Fewer things are harder to put up with than the annoyance of a good example." Can you think of a time recently when you were a good example? A bad example? Can you think of a time when someone else was a bad example?

2. Oswald Chambers wrote, "It is only by obedience that we understand the teaching of God." In what areas do you find it toughest to obey? *Who* do you find toughest to obey?

3. Do you agree that the best sermon is a good example? What are some ways you could preach such a sermon today?

One act of obedience is better than one hundred sermons.
—Dietrich Bonhoeffer (1906–1945)

CHAPTER FIFTEEN

Three Things Dad Did Right

All of us who make motion pictures are teachers—teachers with very loud voices.

—George Lucas, creator of *Star Wars*

When Winston Groom's novel *Forrest Gump* was published in 1986, its heroine was a child of the '60s who sowed some wild oats before finally settling down as a wife and mother. But when the blockbuster movie version was released, a very different Jenny showed up. Drug-addled and suicidal, she eventually got AIDS and died. The reason for her inner turmoil? In one of the film's most unsettling scenes, Forrest watches Jenny throw stones at the already weather-beaten house of her childhood. A house that holds powerful memories of abuse at the hands of her father.

When Jenny finally stops throwing stones and begins to weep, Forrest says, "Sometimes there just aren't enough rocks."

A few days after watching the film, I returned to a small house in my hometown. It stands on the corner of Third

Street and Ninth Avenue, surrounded by poplar trees and its own share of powerful memories. The vacant lot where I first learned to ice skate. The same old sidewalk from which Philip Ewing pulled a big, stringy piece of pink bubble gum. And recycled it.

Across the street someone was pouring concrete beside a large pile of rocks. I realized with a smile that, unlike Jenny, I had no desire to throw them at the house. Then I wondered, *What separates me from the Jennys of my generation?* The answer is simple: My scrapbook is full of memories, but they are happy ones. Some may cause the tears to come, but most bring a smile. Standing in the shade of the poplar trees, I realized how many of those memories involved my father. Three in particular came to mind. Three times an imperfect dad did something right.

He Loved Life's Surprises

I am six. Stevie Graham and I are sitting on the sidewalk, poking bugs with sticks and comparing notes.

"My dad's huger than yours," I say.

"Is not."

"Is so. Plus my dad wrastles tigers."

"Does not."

"Does so."

"Well," he replies, poking me with the stick, "at least my dad wasn't *real old* when I was born. My mom says your dad didn't even want you."

The conversation pretty much ended then, due to the fact that he had no one to talk to. In about three seconds I was in the house crying.

Later, however, I discovered that his words were true. At least partly. Born of parents who were beginning to resemble

Abraham and Sarah (my mother was 36 when she found out about me), I was often referred to as the caboose. Some laughed when they saw Mom waddling toward them on the sidewalk. "What's she doing having another one? Her biological clock is blinking midnight." Some even referred to me as an afterthought. A mistake. But I never heard those words from Dad and Mom. Instead, I heard words like, "I love you," and "I don't know what I'd do without you." And just as importantly, I was shown that love. I was loved, just like the rest.

Today, I admit that Stevie was right about one thing: My father didn't "wrastle" tigers. No, he was much bigger than that. When opportunity knocked, he didn't complain about the noise. He understood that God's grace always accompanies life's surprises.

He Couldn't Spell Very Well

I am eight now. From my bed I can hear the ticktock of the living-room clock. The curious aroma of burnt toast winds its way down the hall. It is early, but suddenly I am wide awake.

This is not just any morning. This is the morning of the hunt.

As we drive down the dusty gravel road this cold November day, I know this will be no ordinary hunting trip. I have been hunting before, but today something is different. Today I am with Dad.

Alone.

Behind us lies the 12-gauge shotgun, brought out on special occasions such as this. In front of us lies what will become one of the most vivid memories of my life.

Being the youngest of five, it is a rare occasion when I can be alone with Dad. He works hard six days a week and travels many weekends. But today he is all mine. Today I am with the greatest hunter in the world. Someone who has not only tracked, but shot, skinned, fried, and eaten an entire pheasant.

Outside, the cold prairie wind brings broad, fluffy snowflakes to rest on the frozen ground, and the last few leaves struggle to release themselves from the grip of the tall poplar trees. But inside our car, the sun is shining.

We enter the forest single file. I am careful not to step on any branches. He is careful not to get too far ahead. Adventure lurks behind every bush. "Sshhh," he says, lifting a finger to his lips. "You never know. . . ." And I am deathly quiet.

We eat our lunch of sandwiches standing in the cold. "Stomp your feet like this," says Dad.

"But won't it scare the rabbits away?"

He smiles in response. "It will keep you warm. Besides, I haven't even seen a rabbit track."

Soon we are on our way home. And although we don't have a trophy to show for our trip, I don't mind.

I have been with the hunter.

Ten years later, we are alone again as we drive down those same dusty roads. The shotgun is in the back seat, but this time it will serve a different purpose. For weeks we have been watching the paper for just the right car. Something old. And something cheap. We have finally found it in the form of a 1970 Ford Maverick, and now we hope to claim the prize.

Arriving at the farmhouse, we carefully examine what will become my very first vehicle. And when it comes time to pay up, Dad takes out his precious shotgun and trades it in.

What made those times with Dad so special? Was it the thrill of the hunt? Or of buying my first car? No. The hunting trip wasn't very successful, and the car has long since rusted. But the memories haven't, because someone who had a "to do" list as long as my arm took the time to be alone with me. Dad couldn't spell very well. He spelled love *t-i-m-e*.

He Loved My Mom

Movie star Jack Nicholson once said, "We should have marriage contracts. Five, ten, fifteen years. It's this forever stuff that throws everything off." Apparently, my dad was never much of a Jack Nicholson fan.

On a snowy December day during World War II, as the temperature dipped to 45 below, he took Mom's hand and made a contract with God. A Canadian corporal on leave, and his 19-year-old bride: "I do take thee . . . for better, for worse, for richer for poorer, in sickness and in health, to love and to cherish till death do us part."

They knew that ten days later the soldier boy would go back to war, leaving his tearful bride waving from a train station platform. And so they joined hands and promised to be faithful. They had no idea their second child would die in their arms or that they would spend their entire lives below the poverty line. But they vowed to comfort each other, no matter what came their way.

Fifty-three years have come along. So have five children and 14 grandchildren. Still the knot is tied tight.

By today's standards, Mom and Dad didn't have much on that cold December day. Just 75 dollars, a solitary wedding ring, and a suitcase full of dreams. Half a century later, they still don't have much. Just a little old mobile home and a car that sometimes runs. But their dreams were never about good fortune. Instead they dreamed of children who would love the Lord—and they got five of them. Instead they dreamed of years of faithfulness—and they got 53 of them. You can travel the world, but I'll guarantee you one thing: You'll never meet wealthier people.

Stepping-Stones

Years ago, a ten-year-old walked into the lingerie department of a clothing store and bashfully informed the clerk that he wanted to buy a slip for his mom. "What size is she?" asked the clerk. "I dunno," replied the boy. The lady lowered her spectacles and explained that it would be helpful if he could describe her—was she fat, thin, short, tall? "Well," the boy replied, "she's just about perfect." So the clerk sent him home with a size 34. The following Monday his mother returned to exchange the gift. Seems it was a little tight. She needed a size 52. According to her boy, however, she was just about perfect.

Now, I've never been tempted to buy a slip for my dad, but I suppose I'm a little like the kid in the lingerie section. I could be accused of sizing things up wrong—of telling stories which paint overly optimistic portraits of my father. The truth is, he made his share of mistakes. But I'd like to spend some time looking on the bright side. After all, pessimism has never been a virtue. If you doubt me, read the following examples:

- A scowling Michigan banker once advised Henry Ford's lawyer not to invest in the new car company. "The horse is here to stay," he told him, "but the automobile is only a novelty."

- In 1895, Lord Kelvin, president of the Royal Society, said with great confidence, "Heavier than air flying machines are impossible."

- In 1899, Charles H. Duell took pessimism to new heights, saying, "Everything that can be invented has been invented."

- Actor Gary Cooper once said, "*Gone With the Wind* is going to be the biggest flop in Hollywood history. I'm just glad it'll be Clark Gable who's falling flat on his face and not me."

I don't know about you, but I'd rather work on solutions than point out problems. I'd rather affect the statistics than analyze them.

Do you feel the same way? Are you tired of hearing what's wrong? Of how badly our parents have messed up our world? Oh, I'm well aware of the problems, but I'm wondering how we'll ever steer this ship in the right direction if all we ever do is stand at the bow discussing yesterday's storms.

Exodus 20:12 (NASB) says, "Honor your father and your mother, that your days may be prolonged in the land which the LORD your God gives you." Increasingly, it is a forgotten commandment. But those who obey it will be rewarded with peace and joy. They will find that rocks are best used as stepping-stones.

Let me encourage you to honor your father. If he is alive, write or call him today. And tell him about the time he did something right. If it's too late, tell someone else about him. Be realistic, but tell them something good. And don't forget that you will be remembered one day. Will your children remember that you loved their mother? That you gave them your time? That you reflected your heavenly Father?

Why not make some memories today?

You may want to begin with a simple hug, an evening at home, or a trip to the country.

You may even want to throw in a shotgun.

Study Guide Questions

Be Honest

1. Martin Luther said, "My own father was hard, unyielding and relentless. I cannot help but think of God that way." How much has your father's life affected your view of God?

2. How good are your memories of your dad? In what ways are you like him? In what ways are you different?

3. What is the last thing you remember saying to someone about your dad?

Go Deep

1. "Rocks are best used as stepping-stones." How have you used the rocks in your life? Is there change needed in this area?

2. "Authentic men," says Charles Swindoll, "aren't afraid to show affection, release their feelings, hug their children, cry when they're sad, admit it when they're wrong, and ask for help when they need it." How are you doing in each of these areas?

3. Ask yourself: How will I be remembered?

4. Before the sun sets, tell someone something good about your dad.

You can't turn back the clock. But you can wind it up again.

—Bonnie Prudden

CHAPTER SIXTEEN

Communication:
The Key to—Among Other Things—
Not Getting Shot

*What do you mean we don't communicate? Just yesterday I
faxed you a reply to the recorded message you left on my
answering machine.*

—*The Wall Street Journal*

We live in the communication age, which, when you stop to
consider that approximately half the population has never
been much good at it, is truly astounding. Yes, I think it's time
we guys admit that as a gender we have occasionally fumbled
big time on the communication field. World history demon-
strates that such fumbles can lead to disaster—a truth vividly
illustrated by the comment Adolph Hitler[1] made to a saluting
stone-faced general: "You invaded *Russia?* You idiot! I said
march through *Prussia!*"[2]

---

[1] Who, amazingly, spoke perfect English when he was really ticked.

[2] Another notorious communication blunder was committed on May 16,
1885, the day Pablo Picasso's father looked at his son's first painting and
said, *"Bueno trabajar, muchacho! Yo semanjante vuestro estilo! Tener el arriba!"*
or "Good job, Pabs. I like your style. I think you should keep it up."

Adolph isn't the only one who has had difficulty communicating. Here are a few classified ads with which postwar guys have cluttered newspapers. Believe me, they are all accurate and unedited. I tried to make some up, but they weren't nearly this good:

> **FOR SALE:** Bulldog. Will eat anything. Loves children.

> **THANKS** to two special people who picked my wife up after a fall from her bike and broke her pelvis and severely damaged her back and many other parts of her body. Jim and Betty Kelleher—there are not enough words to express my gratitude and heartfelt thanks for you and what you did for my wonderful wife.

> **EXTREMELY INDEPENDENT MALE.** 17 years old, needs to rent room. Call his mother at . . .

> **HAVE FAMILY,** would like to exchange for home in Amsterdam.

Or how about this actual transcript of a court "proceeding":

> **LAWYER:** When he went, had you gone and had she, if she wanted to and were able, for the time being excluding all the restraints on her not to go, gone also, would he have brought you, meaning you and she, with him to the station?

> **OPPOSING LAWYER:** Objection. That question should be taken out and shot.

Unfortunately, you don't need a degree in law to succeed at being a lousy communicator. Authors have been known to experience difficulty in this area, too. Take me, for instance.

Typically, I would arrive home from work, kick off my shoes, pick up the newspaper, and hurl myself at the couch, sometimes landing on small children, which caused them to squeal and scatter in various directions. My normally considerate wife would come into the room at this point, aim a rubber band at the front page of the paper, release it—*whaack!*—and ask, "How are you doing?"

"Fine," I would reply.

"How was your day?" she would ask.

"Fine," I would repeat, then turn to page two and try to read around the hole she had made.

"Did anything unusual happen?"

"Nah," I said, growing a little agitated that she would interrupt a perfectly good news story about the possible dangers of mercury fillings to the beaver population—an already endangered species, for Pete's sake—but she persisted in asking district attorney-type questions, grilling me until I had no choice but to set aside the newspaper and recount in vivid detail how my day began like any other day, with breakfast and a quiet time of reading and prayer, but upon my arrival at the office it became apparent that one of the staff—my normally mild-mannered secretary, to be precise—was not in a good mood, judging from the way she pulled a loaded handgun from her purse, took Rosalee (the secretary across the hall) hostage, and began threatening to terminate her employment right there by the coffee station if her demands were not met—demands which included locating washrooms within walking distance of our building, time off on Thanksgiving Day, and upgrading the ribbon in her manual typewriter, but thankfully we were able to hammer out an agreement before noon, which was a good thing because the rest of the day didn't go so smoothly, especially after the weight of all the books in my office became too much for the structure of the building and I plunged ten feet vertically into Dave Epp's office, un-invited, still sitting at my desk, still staring at my computer screen, dust and debris settling all around me.[3]

"We haven't been able to locate Dave yet," I told her, "al-though his wife thinks he's on a business trip somewhere in Iowa, and even if he's not, she says he often shows up late for supper anyway."[4]

"Wow," said Ramona, "That all happened *today?*"

"See, I told you. Everything is fine. Just fine."

She picked up the rubber band. And drilled me between the eyes.

A Few Valuable Lessons

I'd like to think I've learned a few things since that night—a few lessons which have helped keep the communication lines a little more static-free:

- I need to hide my wife's weapons better.

- Seriously, failure to communicate does not just damage countries and newspapers. In fact, many experts[5] believe that the number-one problem in marriages today is not money, sex, or children. It is a lack of communication.

- If you hope to have a truly miserable marriage, charac-terized by (among other things) poor communication, there's one way to mess up your plan: Read the Bible together.

The third one finally did me in. As often as we were able, Ramona and I began reading Scripture together, and I kept

---

[3] Go ahead and take a breath here.

[4] If you're out there somewhere, Dave, please call home.

[5] And even people like myself.

bumping into verses that conflicted with my style. Truths that hit me harder than a dozen rubber bands. I'd be reading along in Ephesians 5, a perfectly harmless chapter, a chapter which contains some guys' life verse ("Wives, submit to your husbands"), and I would be thinking, *Boy, I sure hope she heard that one*, when, suddenly and without warning, we would arrive at verse 25: "Husbands, love your wives, just as Christ loved the church and gave himself up for her. . . ."

A Few More Valuable Lessons

I'll just mention two more things I've learned, because a) I think there's plenty here to think about already, b) I'm still smarting from the rubber band, and c) I've suffered from Attention Deficit Disorder since second grade.

1. *Forget the right stuff.*

Now, let me see . . . what was I going to say here? Oh yes—as you may know, forgetfulness is not always seen as a positive attribute. Just ask Roger Smith, a Presbyterian preacher from Seattle, who has recently gone into hiding. If you're wondering why, I'll tell you.

A few summers ago, Roger was traveling with his family through the Pocono Mountains, and like all good vacationing Presbyterians, they decided to attend church on Sunday. This particular morning was a hot one, and folks in the little Methodist church they attended were nearly passing out in the pews (partly due to the heat and partly due to the fact that the preacher was droning on and on). Suddenly, however, the preacher stopped, cleared his throat, and made an astounding confession: "The best years of my life have been spent in the arms of another man's wife."

As you might suspect, the congregation let out a collective gasp and came to immediate attention. A dozing deacon in the back row dropped his hymnal. Everyone else dropped their jaws.

"It was my mother," concluded the preacher.

A ripple of laughter passed through the congregation, and they managed to follow along as the sermon concluded.

But Roger had trouble listening. Instead, he was making a fateful decision. He was filing this little story into his trusty memory bank under "Just in Case I Ever Lose My Audience." And sure enough, on a lazy Sunday the very next summer, the illustration came in handy.

Roger hadn't been preaching long when he realized that no one was listening. Flies were buzzing. The only ones that appeared to be awake were very small children. Ushers were sinking slowly out of sight. That's when Roger's memory took over for him, and he said in a booming voice, "The best years of my life have been spent in the arms of another man's wife."

He had their attention alright. The congregation stared back with wide eyes and open mouths. One of the ushers in the back row sat up so fast he hit his head on the back of a pew. The flies even quit buzzing. *Ah*, thought Roger, *I've got 'em.*

But something happened then. Something his former parishioners still talk about around tall fires late at night: Roger's memory shorted out. He stood in silence before them, unable to recall the punch line. All he could think to say was, "And for the life of me, I can't remember her name."

I suppose Roger would be the first to admit that forgetfulness is not always an admirable virtue. But I'm sure he would agree that it has its place—like when it is practiced by a congregation.

I have found that my marriage runs more smoothly with a good dose of forgetfulness, too. Elbert Hubbard said, "A retentive memory is a good thing, but the ability to forget is the true token of greatness." He was right. When I refuse to forget petty disagreements, it is amazing how large they become.

Last Christmas, Ramona and I did not speak to each other for approximately two days. It gave "Silent Night" a whole new twist. Do you know how it started? My entrepreneurial son was selling Christmas ornaments door-to-door—ornaments which he had carefully constructed out of pine cones, glue, and long streams of silver tinsel. This was admirable, but when he asked his mother how much he should charge, she told him, "Five cents."

When I heard this, I said, "*Five cents!* He just spent *three hours* building them, and you tell him they're worth *five cents?*" I felt it was an important opportunity to teach the child the value of a buck. After all, we wouldn't want him opening a new-car dealership one day with the campaign slogan: "Real Wheel Deals: 100 Dollars."

Two days later as my wife began sneaking my presents out from under the tree and returning them to fine hardware stores everywhere, the amazing thought hit me: *You know, at one point this really wasn't that big a deal.* Then I remembered Ephesians 4:32: "Be kind and compassionate to one another, forgiving each other, just as in Christ God forgave you."

God is in the business of forgiving and forgetting, I thought. *I'd better be, too.*

The realization led me once again to the six toughest words I'll ever say:[6] "Honey, I'm sorry. I was wrong." As it turned out, she was quick to forgive. She even brought back the presents.

2. *Use your ears more than your mouth.*

Dr. Joyce Brothers once said about her sports-addicted husband, "If we did get a divorce, the only way he would know it is if they announced it on 'Wide World of Sports.'" I hope she wasn't serious. And I sincerely hope things aren't this bad

---

[6] Apart from "Yes, you may marry my daughter."

around your home. If they are, I suggest radical surgery, which would include removal of your retinas. At least you would have your ears left.

The ear is an organ that none of us uses enough. I don't know about you, but I have the tendency to use my mouth much more than my ears—and often before I use my head. It is a common guy problem. So the apostle James was probably thinking of guys like me when he wrote, "Everyone should be quick to listen, slow to speak and slow to become angry" (1:19). Maybe God gave us twice as many ears as tongues for a reason.

Without exception, the best times I spend with my wife, my friends, and my Savior always seem to come along when I listen. Perhaps it wouldn't be all that bad if one day they chiseled these words into my tombstone: "So he didn't live all that long. But hey, he listened."

I do know this: If I spend more time listening, the following epitaph won't be necessary:

Here lies
Philip Ronald Callaway
1961–1996

On top of Old Smokey,
All covered with sand,
He was gunned down while yapping,
By a red rubber band.

Study Guide Questions

Be Honest

1. When you read Dr. Joyce Brothers' words, "If we did get a divorce, the only way he would know it is if they

announced it on 'Wide World of Sports,'" did the words irritate you or make you smile? Was she describing anyone in your house?

2. What do you like to do most when you arrive home from work?

3. Would your spouse say you are a ☐ great ☐ not bad ☐ lousy communicator? Would you like to move into a better category?

4. How well do you listen? ☐ Pretty well ☐ Not so well ☐ I haven't been paying attention—what was the question?

Go Deep

1. Ask yourself: Are there some things my spouse has done recently that I need to forgive? That I need to forget?

2. Practice the following each day: Be a ready listener. Don't use silence to frustrate. Speak the truth in love. When you are wrong, admit it and ask for forgiveness.

3. Read the book of Philippians with your spouse. Then read H. Norman Wright's *Communication: Key to Your Marriage* (Regal Books) together.

A successful marriage is an edifice that must be rebuilt every day.
—André Maurois

CHAPTER SEVENTEEN

The Fright Before Christmas

*There are moments when everything goes well; don't be
frightened, it won't last.*

—Jules Renard (1864–1910)

At our house, in a darkened closet the size of a large casket,
there lurks a creature so scary that adults can't even see
him. But he's there alright. Just ask Jeffrey. Tonight my terri-
fied son stands in the hallway, his heart pounding loudly, his
finger pointing toward the bedroom. "Daddy, come," he beck-
ons. "There's something in there."

On the top bunk, Jeffrey's older brother is grinning widely.
"I told him 'bout the slimy green monster," says Stephen
triumphantly. "He's scared."

I know the feeling. Older brothers lurked in my childhood
too. And so, ever eager to comfort my sons, I decided to tell them
a horror story—paraphrasing it, of course, for younger ears. . . .

When I was 12, my mother would wait until dusk before sending me to the cellar to retrieve cans of applesauce from a box which never seemed to run dry. This was 20 years ago, before the invention of light switches as we know them. All we had in those primitive years were pull cords hanging from dark basement ceilings, and heartless electricians ensured that none of them were ever conveniently placed.

A few days before Christmas, my older brother Tim warned me "just so's I would be careful" of a creature who had found shelter in our cellar. As I listened wide-eared, he described a white-fanged wolverine the size of an eighth-grader that enjoyed little children and craved applesauce. "Sometimes you can see his yellow eyes before he grabs you," cautioned Tim. "But mostly he keeps 'em shut 'til it's too late."

With a hoarse whisper I asked him why he hadn't done something about it, him being so big and all. He claimed he had. In fact, he had bludgeoned the beast himself with a rake and buried it in a grove of fir trees. But that only served to anger the wolverine community. One by one they had come out of hiding to dwell in our cellar and seek vengeance. There were three of them down there now, he thought. Maybe a whole herd. "Them that are eaten shall have no Christmas," said he.

I did not sleep that night for pondering his words. To the child who is afraid, everything squeaks.

"Philip." It was Christmas Eve, and Mother needed applesauce. Tiptoeing obediently down the stairway and into the lengthening shadows, I agreed to serve God in obscure countries. "Just get me to that first 40-watt light bulb," I prayed earnestly.

With renewed strength, I strode boldly toward it, tripped over a toolbox, and whacked my forehead on the Ping-Pong table.

I don't remember much about the next few seconds.

In fact, certain details from the next few years are still a little sketchy. Dates. Faces. My name. But apparently I located the light bulb, because I recall standing beneath it, trying to regain my balance and switch off my fears.

Then came the cellar.

The hinges on our cellar door were seldom oiled, and the sound of them turning only added to the suspense. Timidly, I entered the room.

The dim light above the Ping-Pong table threw ghostly images against the far wall, but the rest of the room was shrouded in darkness. Six steps to my right past a box of whiskered potatoes was the pull cord. I walked slowly toward it and reached out my hand.

There are defining moments in all of our lives. Moments that sound reason may block out as we grow older. Moments that good psychiatrists are trained to help us recall.

This was mine.

As I took hold of the pull cord, I felt instead something cold, wet, and slimy. And as I screamed, I beheld the one thing I feared the most: A PAIR OF YELLOW EYES.

Racing around the Ping-Pong table, I hurdled the toolbox. Scrambling up the stairway, I heard the laughter. It was coming from behind me. It was coming from my brother. Yes, Tim was there. Holding two flashlights. And an empty can of spaghetti.

"Did that really happen?" asks Stephen.

"Well, everything except the spaghetti. I threw that in there to watch your eyes get big."

"Uncle Tim was mean," he says.

"Sometimes big brothers are. But he's one of my best friends today."[1]

"So Christmas was the very next day?"

"Yes, it was. And I think it was the best one yet. You see, if you've ever been afraid of the basement or your big brother, if you've ever been afraid of darkness or death, there's nothing quite like the message of Christmas to turn the lights on. *Immanuel, God is with us.*

"His presence brings peace for today and bright hope for tomorrow. Those who fear Him have nothing to be afraid of."

Jeffrey seems to have found comfort in my words. He is sound asleep. But not Stephen. He is wide awake. Very wide awake. An older brother with his eyes fixed firmly on the closet.

Study Guide Questions

Be Honest

1. Did older siblings lurk in your basement? Have you forgiven them?

---

[1] When a shortened version of this story was published in *Servant* magazine, Tim faxed me the following letter, which we published in the letters section. Unfortunately, a few readers took it seriously:

> As the editor's older brother, I must protest his indiscriminate usage of sensitive family historical data in "The Fright Before Christmas." Bringing to light an incident I had long since suppressed into the nether regions of my dysfunctional subconsciousness forces me to consider returning to therapy so that I might ponder similar memories arising from a completely normal childhood. I don't have time for such pursuits. Besides, is Phil prepared to subsidize the cost of such treatments?

2. Did you like scaring people when you were a kid? What was so fun about it? Do you still like scaring people?

3. Why do you think people enjoy horror movies? Do you?

4. How many of the things you fear can you control?

Go Deep

1. Think back to a time when you were really scared. Now, get into a really dark room, shine a flashlight on your face and tell small children about it. Just kidding—but if your kids are afraid, tell them about a time when you were, too. Tell them what helped you.

2. Think for a minute—what frightens you the most? Why?

3. "Those who fear God have nothing to be afraid of." Do you agree? What does it mean to fear God?

4. Read Psalm 128:1; Proverbs 1:7; 8:13; Isaiah 35:4; 43:1.

5. Frances J. Roberts wrote, "Relinquishment of burdens and fears begins where adoration and worship of God become the occupation of the soul." Spend some time thanking God for who He is.

6. Memorize the following:

So do not fear, for I am with you; do not be dismayed, for I am your God. I will strengthen you and help you; I will uphold you with my righteous right hand.

—Isaiah 41:10

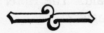

CHAPTER EIGHTEEN

Disappointment with Christians

*The world is not a prison house, but a kind of spiritual
kindergarten where millions of bewildered infants are
trying to spell God with the wrong blocks.*

—Edwin Arlington Robinson

Recently I received a phone call from a non-Christian friend.
"Hey, Phil," he said, "I've got an extra ticket for Friday's
concert. You wanna go?"

"Sure, Frank," I said. "Is that the George Beverly Shea
concert?"

"George Beverly *who?*"

"Oh, he's a great old singer my mom used to play when I
was a kid. Who's in town Friday night? It's not that cool new
group 'I Can't Take It Anymore So I'll Just Smash Pumpkin-
heads,' is it?"

Thankfully, Frank laughed. "Naw, it's the Eagles. They're
old and balding. You'll be able to relate." Frank gets like this
when he hasn't eaten lunch.

"The Eagles?" I said. "The Hotel California, New Kid in Town, Take It Easy, Eagles?"

"That's them."

"So," I asked, "are the tickets, like . . . free, or do they take up an offering?"

"They're 75 bucks," he said.

"Sorry," I said, laughing, "for a minute there I thought you said 75 bucks."

"I did."

"So is that per *row?*" I asked.

"Per *seat*," he replied.

"Uh, I'd better consult my wife on this one."

"Sure, I think you should go for it," said Ramona after picking herself up off the floor. "We'll be okay. I'll send the kids door-to-door with collection plates until month end. Seriously," she added, "I'm glad you can spend some time with Frank."

Frank King and I first shared pizza on a cool spring day in 1993. We were a curious pair: he, a polished member of the secular media, and I, a Christian magazine editor. Two years earlier we were acquainted through Frank's weekly music review column in the Religion section of a large metropolitan daily newspaper. I read with interest his views, and on occasion found myself agreeing with his verdicts. When I phoned to tell him so, our friendship began.

"I'm not a Christian," Frank explained up front. "At least not anymore."

"Why don't we talk about it?" I responded. "I'll be in the city tomorrow. You can tell me what bugs you about Christians."

"Boy," laughed Frank, "you're really asking for it."

So it was that we found ourselves sharing an outdoor table, some mediocre pizza, and a fascinating conversation.

"Don't you pray or something before we start?" he asked as we sat down. I smiled, then prayed out loud, thanking God for pizza and new friendships. Then I asked Frank about his spiritual pilgrimage.

"Well, I grew up in a good Catholic home," he began. "About three years ago, I had what you would call a 'salvation experience.' But since then too many questions have gone unanswered. I've seen too many hypocrites."

On the lawn nearby, Frank's coworkers exercised their frustrations in three–on–three volleyball. Overhead, gray clouds dispersed and the midday sun poked through. As I peeled off my spring jacket, Frank began to pour out his thoughts.

I listened.

"Apologists say Christianity is a thinking person's faith," he continued, talking partly with his hands. "But in my travels, I've seen a disturbing number of believers—especially evangelicals—who have stopped thinking. Time and time again when I mention some burning issue, I'm met by blank stares from my Christian friends. Time and time again I've had to explain what's going on, and why it should matter to them as fellow citizens of planet Earth."

Frank paused for a moment. "This one's controversial," he smiled, "but I'm amazed at how Christians treat those who are homosexual. When I tried explaining to a close Christian friend the theory that most of these people are born with their sexual identities, rather than acquiring them, she came right out and compared homosexuality to murder. Whether the theories are right or wrong, she seemed unable or unwilling to consider the issue. Was Jesus not the living embodiment of compassion? Did He not spend His time with the outcasts of society? I'm not suggesting He approved of their behavior, but based on His actions, would He not extend extraordinary love to today's outcasts?"

A stray volleyball rolled under our table. Frank picked it up and bounced it back. "The way I see it," he said, "following Christ's words means thinking and praying long and hard about what you believe and why. It also means reading books (not just Christian ones) and newspapers, learning about other faiths, taking the time to consider who you're voting for and why. I realize thinking can create uncomfortable moments when people realize they don't know why they believe something. Nevertheless, thinking Christians are a powerful elixir to those of us who have difficulty with the faith's basic concepts."

The volleyball game had ended by this time. My half of the pizza was gone. And as Frank talked, I thought of my own disappointment with Christians. Of the ones who would wince at Frank's generous expletives yet be blind to the greater sin of their own gossip and backbiting. Of the first day on a job trying to figure out why I was being yelled at by a fellow believer. *I've rarely seen God while looking at people,* I thought. A. W. Tozer's words came to mind: "There is nothing so refreshing as to watch a new Christian before he has heard too many sermons and watched too many Christians." Was this partly why Jesus was often found in the company of prostitutes and sinners? Those who had nothing to hide?

"I guess I'm coming across a little heavy-handed." Frank had noticed my faraway look.

"No, not at all. I was just thinking. . . . I like your honesty."

The clouds converged on the sun again. I slipped on my jacket, and Frank moved to the heart of the matter. "I'm told that the Holy Spirit dwells in the heart in a symbolic sense. A pastor friend told me that the Spirit illuminates the Word of God, convicts, draws people to Christ, and reveals Him to them. But most believers blatantly ignore His guidance about the need to embrace rather than judge people.

"Every time a Christian from one denomination puts down another denomination or another Christian, I feel glad I'm not affiliated with people who talk the walk of unity but have no interest in walking the talk. Am I wrong to suggest the Holy Spirit wants Christians to concentrate on all the common ground and let God deal with the rest? Instead I see churches splitting over which translation of the Bible is to be used or what style of worship is best. Didn't Christ say that the world would know who you were by your love? Didn't He say, 'However you judge, so shall you be judged'? Shouldn't Christians treat that Scripture with a great deal of seriousness?"

I nodded my head, yet said little that afternoon. Perhaps it was best. As we stood to leave, I remembered how I had prayed that God would help me know what to say. I wondered now if He was more interested in saying something to me—through Frank. "Christians should make all of Christianity the basis for their lives," he said. "In short, know what you believe, why you believe it, then live it."

On the night of the concert, we sat for three hours, surrounded by aging baby boomers, watching the Eagles soar through the last few decades. For three hours I was back in high school. My toes were tapping. My fingers snapping. For a few minutes, I even thought I had hair. The tour would earn the boys a record 63.3 million dollars, and it comforted me to know that I was able to have some small part in it. After all, as I pointed out to Frank, these guys have to feed their kids.

The most memorable moment in the concert came near the end of the evening, when Joe Walsh stepped forward and played a mellow slide-guitar solo. The song had been a hit long before the new kid was in town. Long before anyone in the audience was born.

> Amazing grace how sweet the sound,
> That saved a wretch like me.
> I once was lost but now am found,
> Was blind but now I see.

Surprisingly, most of the 16,000 people present sang along. Frank and I joined them.

Following our pizza dinner, we talked often on the phone, discussing music, apologetics, theology, and personal relationships. It was on the latter that we connected most often. Frank was struggling through the pain of a promising relationship gone sour when we met unexpectedly one day and sat down to discuss the events of the past year. "I'm in another relationship now," he said. "She's a great girl, but to be honest, I'm not sure if I love her."

I told him about my marriage of 11 years. How it could not be described as perfect. How we had struggled at times, but how the storms had served to strengthen it, bringing us closer and deepening our relationship. I told him about my faith in Jesus Christ. That, although I believe I know the Answer, I still have some questions for Him. I reminded him that Jesus is the only sinless One. That Christians like me fall short.

When I finished, Frank looked at me with tears in his eyes. "You know that Foreigner song, 'I wanna know what love is'? That's my song. I would give anything for that kind of love."

His words were not what I expected. But they made sense. You see, a watching world needs to see that faith and reason go hand in hand. They need to see guys who put obedience into action. But more, they need to see our love.

That night I told Frank that I would pray for him. That he would find that love. And I breathed a silent prayer for myself, that I would not stand in the way of the One who wants to show it to him.

Study Guide Questions

Be Honest

1. Do you have any non-Christian friends? If not, why? If you do, what kind of example are you? Are you trying to evangelize them or love them?

2. Did any of Frank's comments upset you? Why?

3. Rebecca Manley Pippert said, "Christians and non-Christians have something in common: We're both uptight about evangelism." How uptight are you?

Go Deep

1. Oswald Chambers asked a question which each of us should consider: "How many people have you made homesick for God?" What do you think he meant?

2. According to Henry Ward Beecher, "You never know till you try to reach them how accessible men are; but you must approach each man by the right door." What opportunities does your line of work open up for you in this area?

3. "By this all men will know that you are my disciples, if you love one another" (John 13:35). What will it take for you to be known by your love?

> *Being an extrovert isn't essential to evangelism—obedience and love are.*
>
> —Rebecca Manley Pippert

CHAPTER NINETEEN

Speechless in Seattle

How can you say my life is not a success? Have I not for more than sixty years got enough to eat and escaped being eaten?

—Logan Pearsall Smith (1865–1946)

It's surprising the things that flash through your mind when you're about to die.

Recently, my wife and I were sitting in Seattle's International Airport, eating plywood-flavored burritos that bore little resemblance to the advertisements on the wall, and wondering which would be quicker: waiting for our connecting flight home or crawling the remaining 2000 miles uphill on fiberglass insulation.

As you may have sensed by now, I'm not real fond of air travel. In fact, I believe that Orville and Wilbur should have left well enough alone—the world was a smoother place before turbulence. Yes, I know God's promise, "Lo, I am with you always," but does the verse say anything about what happens when you leave the ground? I think not.

So each time I fly, I update my insurance policy, revamp my will, make things right with friends and loved ones, then climb aboard, hoping for a seat next to an aeronautics engineer, a physicist, or a politician—anyone who will give me a satisfactory answer to the question that has plagued mankind since the very advent of flight: Why does food taste so bad at 30,000 feet?

On this particular day, Ramona and I were herded on board, strapped into tiny seats, catapulted six miles into space, and still we didn't crash. So they brought us back down, put us on a different plane, and gave it another shot. Finally, they requested that we sit in Seattle waiting to do it all over again.

The evening news droned overhead as we reclined in leatherish airport seats, thankful that all four feet were finally on solid ground.

We're safe, I thought. *Nothing can go wrong in an airport.*

Sitting there wondering what to do with the burrito, I replayed the last few days. We had spent them in sunny California, where I had been interviewed for a job with a well-known corporation.[1] I would like to say that the salary offer of almost three times my current wage had little to do with my decision to step aboard an airplane, but it would be a bold-faced lie. The truth is, I was flattered. I was staring down the sights of opportunity. A bigger house. A newer car. Prestige. Success.

All I had to do was squeeze the trigger.

During the interview, I asked—among other things—a few questions on the subject of travel. "How many days a month will I be on the road?"

There was silence.

They looked at me as if I were from the planet Krypton. Finally, someone said, "The question isn't how much

---

[1] A special thanks to the family and former friends who babysat for us.

you'll be gone, Phil. It's how much you'll be home. But keep in mind . . . this kind of work has its own rewards."

Ramona was sitting with me for that part of the interview, with a wrinkled look on her face, and on the flight into Seattle she had held my white knuckles and expressed her concern. "We live in a small town where God has given you a rewarding ministry . . . you have a young family . . . we'd really like to see you occasionally. . . ."

But as I stood to deliver the burrito to a nearby garbage can, I renewed my determination to take the job. The offer was too good to refuse. I would call California from home—if our connecting flight ever arrived.

Overhead, the intercom interrupted my thoughts. "There's bad weather *crackle*," it said. "Flights *crackle . . . crackle* are experiencing delays, however *crackle* is departing immediately from Gate *crackle*."

I left Ramona and went looking for someone who could decipher airport code. No, they told me, our plane had not yet landed. No, they did not know when it would. And no, I could not have any more of those little packages of peanuts.

A little frustrated, I headed for the restroom, entered a tiny stall, and latched the door behind me.

Suddenly, the place began to shake like the bridge of the starship Enterprise. The lights flickered. The door rattled on its hinges. The walls shook.

I knew immediately that there were three possibilities: a) an earthquake, b) a meteorite, c) the burritos.

But as the place continued to shake, I eliminated the latter two. Yes, for the first time in my life I was in the middle of an earthquake. And to make matters worse, I was going to die.

Now I don't know if you've thought much about dying, or if you've ever compiled a list of the top ten places in which you would most like to pass from this refrain to the next, but

I suspect a Seattle International Airport washroom does not figure high on that list.

During the next few seconds, brief memories flashed before me in vivid Technicolor: The time I awoke to my father's worried face after being knocked out on a hockey rink. The day my brother bought me a vanilla ice-cream cone for no reason at all. The miraculous birth of our first child. Faces of friends. Family. My wife. My kids.

From the stall next to mine came a deep but cheerful voice: "Did I do that?"

I was speechless.

Frantically, I unlatched the door and ran from the room. Desperately I hoped to catch a final glimpse of my wife before being encased in rubble. Ah, to hold her in my arms. To kiss her deeply. To let her feel the earth move one last time.

But by now I was the only one running. The rattling had stopped. The quake had ended. *Apparently folks around here are accustomed to such episodes*, I thought. *Perhaps they even like them.*

> *Husband:* Honey, do you mind rubbing my neck? I'm feeling a little tense tonight.
>
> *Wife:* Sure, just as soon as I rearrange this furniture.
>
> *Earthquake:* Rattle, Shake.
>
> *Husband:* Ah, that's better. Forget about the neck rub, dear. I'm fine.
>
> *Wife:* Hey, the furniture looks good, too.

Fellow travelers stared at me with odd expressions, so I slowed down and jogged casually the rest of the way—a stressed-out traveler in need of exercise.

"Did you feel that, Honey?" I had reached my destination, stirred and shaken. "That . . . that rattling?"

"Ya, I think our plane just arrived," she smiled. "I think it landed on the roof."

Five minutes later the evening news confirmed the reality of the quake. It registered 5.0 on Mr. Richter's scale. And a little higher on mine.

I guess earthquakes have a way of shattering your idea of what's important. I guess a brush with death has a way of reminding you what matters most in life. On the final leg of our journey, an interesting question hit me: *Why am I so tempted to steal time from those who care for me the most and give it to those who care the least?*

Upon our safe arrival home, I found a growing pile of mail on my desk. In one envelope was a note from my mother. It was written only days earlier, but it contained a paragraph penned almost 200 years ago by my great, great, great, great grandfather.

Listen to the words he wrote for his grandchildren in 1817:

> Let me entreat you to live near to God, to choose Him for your portion. I would rather hear of your having an interest in Christ than in any possession the world can afford. The joys, the pleasures, the riches, and the honors the world can afford are fleeting and transitory, passing away like the dew in the morning or the shadows which surround you. True wisdom affords riches which are durable, pleasures which are lasting, honors which are permanent, and joys that never fail. . . . May you be useful members of society, blessings to all

around you, and in a good old age fall asleep in Jesus, and awake to a glorious and happy immortality.

Signed,

John Chester Williams
Vermont, September 23, 1817

Further down the pile of mail I found quite a contrast. It was on the back cover of a colorful brochure from one of the fastest-growing businesses today. There a salesman was pictured beside his brand-new swimming pool. When asked what it would take for him to consider himself a success, he answered: "When you see a Porsche 911 in my driveway."

His comment got me wondering about my own definition, so I sat down, pushed the brochure aside, and wrote the following words:

- I will consider myself a success when I am walking close to Jesus every day.

- I will consider myself successful when I am building a strong marriage, loving my kids, and performing meaningful work.

- I will consider myself a success when I am infecting others with the love of Jesus.

To this day I have nothing against a higher salary, a bigger home, or a fancier car. But true success won't be found there. It will be found in seeking, loving, and obeying God. Take my word on this one—or fly to Seattle and check it out yourself.

Study Guide Questions

Be Honest

1. Was there a time in your life when you thought you were going to die? What went through your mind? Why?

2. Do you share the author's fear of flight? Why or why not? Do you think the author should get counseling?

3. Are you tired of climbing the ladder of success—of keeping your nose to the grindstone, your shoulder to the wheel, your eye on the ball, your ear to the ground, and your ducks in a row?

4. Have you told anyone about your struggles in this area?

Go Deep

1. Ask yourself: What would it take for me to consider myself successful? How do I define true success? Write down your answers.

2. Are you at a crossroads in your life? In your work? Have you sought the advice of godly men and women? Have you prayed about it? Have you examined your motives? Have you read God's Word for guidance? What else should you do?

3. Name five things that matter most to you. How many of them involve relationships?

4. Answer the following questions:
   - Am I walking close to Jesus today?
   - Am I doing anything to build a stronger marriage today?

- Can my kids tell that I love them?
- Am I performing meaningful work?
- Am I walking in integrity?
- Will I infect anyone with the love of Jesus today?

5. Ask yourself: If a building fell in on me today, would I go to heaven? How do I know? Who would attend my funeral?

6. Is the planet a better place because I'm on it?

A man leaves all kinds of footprints when he walks through life. Some you can see, like his children and his house. Others are invisible, like the prints he leaves across other people's lives: the help he gives them and what he has said—his jokes, gossip that has hurt others, encouragement. A man doesn't think about it, but everywhere he passes, he leaves some kind of mark.

—Margaret Lee Runbeck

CHAPTER TWENTY

Surprise Beginnings

A small town is a place where there's no place to go where you shouldn't.

—Burt Bacharach

Every Thursday evening we could hear him. The Christian Answer Guy. He came into our living room just after nine and stayed until eleven. Or until someone got real mad and turned the dial.

In the early days, before the show went national, its only venue was our tiny town of Moose Jaw, Idaho, and almost everyone listened. Radio doesn't get better than a talk show where you know every caller. In some cases it was a blessing. Like the time Chuck Burns called to explain why he'd just shot his neighbor's German Shepherd, Patch. The whole town held its breath when the neighbor got through to give his side of the story, and before long the two were both on the air, reconciling, and the town was breathing again.

It wasn't always a blessing though.

One night Mrs. Wiens called, thoroughly upset that the show's name seemed to exclude women callers. "You haven't heard the last from me," she said in a prophetic moment. Two nights later, on a day we'll never forget, the studio burned to the ground and the police surrounded the Wiens home and the whole town knew that sometimes radio can take you too far.

On a typical evening, though, after they rebuilt the studio and jailed Mrs. Wiens, things were a little more normal. Well, maybe not. You be the judge.

"Good evening faithful listeners (catchy background music fades to foreground). It's the Christian Answer Guy with you for another hour of our popular weekly broadcast, "Guy Talk," addressing the needs and concerns of guys everywhere.

"During the first hour we were talking with Howard Smeltzner, local author of *The Wounded Buck: Tales of the Uxorious*. I was going to ask Howie how he balances his busy schedule with family time, but his wife called during the news and he had to leave us a little early. So, I think I'll just throw the phone lines open. You can reach us by dialing . . . uh . . . well . . . I guess Howie took the cue cards, too. Just look us up in the phone book and dial the number. You're in touch and in tune with Radio WXYZ. Hey, looks like we've got a call already. Hello, caller one? Go ahead."

"Uh, hi, it's Arthur Baxter. Is Sharon there?"

"Arthur, I think you've got the wrong number. This is radio station WXYZ. You're on live."

(Dead air) "Uh, oh . . . Mom, if you're listening, I was just going to ask Sharon about the Math assignment . . . oh shoot."

(Click.)

"Well, let me see . . . we have another caller on the line. Go ahead, please. You're on 'Guy Talk' with the Christian Answer Guy."

"Hello," twangs a nasal voice. "Um . . . I'm a first-time caller . . . and I'm really nervous. I was just wondering if . . . well . . . you could give me some advice. I've . . . um . . . been married now for two years and we have two kids and things aren't going too hot."

"Well, for starters, Reg, everyone knows who you are, so you might as well take the clothespin off your nose. You're in the company of friends, you know."

"Uh, all right."

"So things aren't going too smooth for you and Edna, is that right?"

"Yes. I mean, no, they're really not."

Everyone listening knows Reg and Edna. They grew up together in Moose Jaw, where Reg has worked as a maintenance man since the day he turned 16. It was said that Edna hadn't really noticed Reginald until the day he was washing windows just outside the third and final floor of our small town's only skyscraper. When Edna stepped off the elevator looking for her optometrist, she hadn't put in her contact lenses yet, and she saw only a blur which was Reginald, silhouetted against a murky sky, waving hairy hands in concentric circles. Edna thought he was signaling for help and her natural instincts took over. Kicking off her high heels, she crawled out on the ledge, her short red hair bouncing in the stiff breeze. Lunging onto the scaffold, she embraced Reginald tightly, and realized who he was—just plain old Reginald—the one whose love she had spurned since kindergarten, for reasons she couldn't recall. Edna liked what she saw, but made the mistake of stepping back to admire him. Three days later she woke up in the local hospital with stars in her eyes.

They married a month later. Tonight, Reg was wishing she'd never seen those stars. He was wishing he'd stayed up on that scaffold and finished the job.

"So what seems to be the problem, Reg?"

"Well, a lot of things, I guess. You know, someone gave us this wedding gift, this really nice framed list of suggestions. I guess it was a joke, but I hung it in our bathroom. And I've done about everything on that list."

"Do you have the list there, Reg? Can you read it to us?"

"I'll go get it."

While Reg goes down the hall the whole town comes to attention. Mr. McCarthy crawls out from under his '56 Plymouth Belvedere, the one with the push-button gear shift, and turns up the volume. Mrs. Wiens tells the other inmates to be quiet. You could cut the suspense with a knife there in the prison—if you could get your hands on one. Finally, Reg is back, list in hand, reading it clearly over the airwaves:

Twenty–five ways to grieve your lover

1. Fill the medicine cabinet with marbles.

2. Take your bike apart in the living room.

3. Ask her why she can't program the VCR.

4. Tell her to breathe evenly while she's giving birth.

5. Tell her anything while she's giving birth.

6. Become a golfaholic.

7. Take her golfing. Cheer as she putts.

8. Get a dog. Say you'll potty train it.

9. Get a kid. Say you'll potty train it.

10. Remind her that certain African women have their children during coffee breaks.

11. For her birthday, buy her weigh scales for the bathroom.

12. Do your own plumbing.

13. Fill the fridge with marbles.

14. Eat apples in bed. Loudly.

15. Plan a potluck without her present.

16. Leave the toilet seat off.

17. Jog in the house.

18. Without getting her opinion, buy a blue sofa.

19. Without getting her opinion, invite relatives for Christmas.

20. Without getting her opinion, invite 10 boys to a birthday party—in January.

21. Spend more than you make.

22. Glue the remote control to your hand.

23. If you have toddlers, ask her what she did today.

24. Clip her toenails while she's sleeping.

25. Remind her that it is the female mosquito that bites.

When Reg finishes reading, there is only silence. Finally the host says, "You mean you've done everything on that list, Reginald?"

"Yep," whispers Reg regretfully.

The host turns down the mic. But you can still hear him laughing. Finally he recovers long enough to say, "Well, friends, I think it's time some of you older guys called in with some better advice. Maybe we could even frame it for him. Whaddya say?"

Seconds later the switchboard lights up. I sit by the radio for the next half hour, frantically taking notes. Here's what I write:

Twenty–five ways to please your lover

1. After you locate the clothes basket, begin putting your underwear in it.

2. Live by the rule: Last one out of bed makes it.

3. Forgive her 490 times, then stop keeping track.

4. When she hugs you, be the last to let go. (Don't carry this too far, guys.)

5. Ask her a question, then listen to the answer.

6. If you are old enough to shave, you're old enough to clean the shavings.

7. Let your first words each day be kind ones.

8. Stop blaming others.

9. Don't gossip.

10. Don't major on the minors.

11. Sometimes take out the garbage without being told.

12. Forget keeping up with the Joneses.

13. Leave the TV off more.

14. Dance with her in the living room. Sometimes include the children.

15. Praise publicly; criticize privately.

16. Keep your promises.

17. Never overestimate your power to change your wife.

18. Never underestimate your power to change yourself.

19. Get more exercise.

20. Encourage her.

21. Read the Bible together.

22. Pray together.

23. Be a thankful person.

24. Look through the windshield more than the rearview mirror.

25. Put God first.

The last call of the evening comes from Edna.

She wants to thank everyone for their advice and she says that Reg isn't the only problem. That she's made some mistakes in her life, too. "Things are gonna change, though," she promises.

And as the music fades into the night, I think everyone believes her.

There are tears in Edna's eyes as she hangs up the phone. "It's okay, Mrs. Wiens," the officer says, handing her a hanky. "You'll be released Monday. You get another chance."

To this day you can see murky stains on the third floor window of Moose Jaw's only skyscraper. Reg has never taken the time to scrub them off. No one seems to mind, though. In fact, I believe the whole town wants them there. I think the stains remind us all of God's grace and mercy. Of forgiveness. Of making the best of what you have. I think they remind us that it's never too late to start again.